MW00412847

Silly Shorts

Cover Design by Stephen Prestek
PRINT ISBN: 9781731402943

Silly Shorts

By Ginger O. Snap

This book is dedicated to anyone who has ever felt a little sad or lonely.

I hit rock bottom in 2008
and woke up immobilized by the blues.
I knew I must have had
one happy time in my lifetime.
When I remembered that one time
and wrote it down, I felt better.
I hope this book helps you feel better.

Acknowledgements

Without the tireless support of my best friend Brenda June Vanderhoff, this book would not exist. When I had been turned down for five years for airline jobs, she believed in me and drove from Seattle to Houston with me when I was hired by Continental Airlines. When I started college at forty with a one-year-old baby and cranky husband, she encouraged me to hang in there, working all day and going to night school for five years. When I couldn't get hired as a teacher at fifty because I was too old, Brenda encouraged me when I decided to go to librarian school. The moral of this story is you only need one friend who believes in you. Thank you Brenda.

Contents

Chapter One

The Femailman

Sure I Had Mace

I did use mace once. I was delivering mail along Magnolia Boulevard on a sunny spring day, in 1978. As I walked past some low box hedges to a big red brick house, a tiny wiener doggy shot out of nowhere and nipped my ankle. I grabbed my Mace and sprayed him. I turned that protective little dog into a monster! Every day for the rest of that week, I'd be walking along, lost in my " Get the Right Mail in The Right Box" world, and the tiny Monster Dog would be hiding under the box hedge waiting to attack me. I hated that. When I was assigned a new route down along the flats of Magnolia, I got nervous. I had driven down 34th Avenue West on my way back to the tiny post office on West McGraw and noticed tons of dogs. Big dogs. Not the tiny designer dogs of the rich people. My first day on the route, a huge golden lab barked at me as I approached his house. I knew golden labs were friendly but I had a surprise for him. I tossed him a Milk Bone. He started following me up the street. Then his friends showed up, and I gave them ALL Milk Bones. Every day for two weeks I had six dogs following me, up one side of the street, and down the other. Sure I had mace. But it was way more fun being the Pied Piper of Magnolia!

Sitka and the Jelly Doughnut

When I think back to my ten years of carrying mail, what pops into my head is dogs. Dogs growling at me, trying to bite me, dogs biting me... Well, you get the picture. When Gary had his hernia surgery, I was lucky enough to be assigned Route 17. After being on a different mail route every day for six months, three months on the same route in beautiful Bothell was like going on a vacation. My first day on his route, I was near the end up on 212th SW when this huge white dog came charging at my mail jeep. All fur and teeth and ready to shred me. I threw the mail in the box and shoved up my window. This happened every day for two months! One Friday afternoon I arrived with the mail in one hand and a jelly doughnut in the other. I was in my "Get the Right Mail in the Right Box" world when the dog charged me. Startled, I threw my doughnut at the ferocious dog. Said dog, opened wide and caught the doughnut in its mouth. Then The Dog quit barking, sat down, and started wagging its tail. The following day was hot, and I was getting miserable. I opened the door on my little mail-jeep, to cool off. Driving with your door open is a huge no no. I have two friends that have accidentally fallen out. So I arrived near The Dog's house and The Dog Owner Man is pulling weeds in his front yard and his pony of a dog is sleeping on the front porch. Next thing I know, The Dog is sitting on my lap, in the mail jeep, licking my face. The Dog Owner Man walks over with an astonished expression and says, "Wow! Sitka doesn't usually like ANYBODY!"

Hop In Mr Simpson

I delivered plenty of strange things during my ten years on the mail routes. In the blistering summer of 1980, I had just finished “Putting the Right Mail in the Right Box”, when I looked in my mirror and saw Mr. Simpson coming up the hill. He looked terrible! I jumped out of my jeep and ran to him and could tell he had heat exhaustion. He told me he had walked from Holly Hills down to the Woodinville Dairy Queen for lunch and didn't feel good. Well, duh! It was almost ninety degrees out! I opened the back of my mail jeep, moved my empty trays and said, "Hop in, Mr. Simpson." He pretzeled up his huge six-foot frame into the back of my tiny jeep and off we went the ten blocks to his house. I pulled up to the house and opened the jeep door and dashed up his driveway and got Irene. "Mrs. Simpson,” I said, "I have a special delivery for you." We went down and I opened the back of my jeep and we each took an arm and helped Mr. Simpson up to the house and I went on my merry way. Mr. Simpson was possibly my strangest delivery and I forgot to collect Postage Due for the delivery!

Snake In The Box

People that know me well, know that I am jumpy. They approach me slowly, waving their arms from a bit of an angle to make sure I see them. Otherwise they know I'm prone to shrieking. I do that when surprised or startled, or both. I don't know why God made me this way but I do know that it disturbs people. I am a sociable, outgoing person. Just a bit jumpy that's all. So you can just imagine what happened when I was cruising up Holly Hills Avenue in my mail jeep, and I opened the mailbox door and there was a snake sitting about a foot from my face. Who knew garter snakes could coil up? I hadn't ever looked at one from eye level before. I didn't know that they had really sharp looking fangs, and that their tongues are split and wave horizontally. Too much information! I shrieked and threw the mail up in the air and it landed all over the ground. Surprisingly, I didn't crash my jeep. I managed to pull ahead of the big wooden double mailbox stand and park my jeep. I got out and stood their shaking in my sturdy black femailman shoes, and blue uniform. Mr. Isenhour came out to see what the commotion was, and I showed him the snake, which hadn't budged. He pulled it out, put it in the yard, then picked up all the mail and put it in the boxes for me. Like the dogs weren't bad enough!

Odd Things In My Mail Jeep

I shoved the last letters into their tiny one-inch slots on my sorting case and hustled over to my parcel bin. A coconut! I couldn't believe it and started laughing. I did not know you were allowed to mail mail that didn't look like mail. After a few years of delivering mail in Seattle out of Magnolia, Bitter Lake and North City, I was able to get hired at Bothell post office as a substitute. After five years as a sub and one long year as a T-6, I reached the epitome of postalhood. My own route! Beautiful Holly Hills mobile estates was mine, mine, mine. Gary, the man I inherited the route from told me, "There's old in them hills!" The people were all retired and it was fun to see them at their mailboxes every day. Mr. Powell was building a mail order car. Yes, you read right! Mr. Powell joined a "Build-A-Car" club and every week for three years I delivered a new part. The seven-foot exhaust pipe just barely fit in my tiny mail jeep. Every week I'd deliver a new part. The six-foot mid-pipe that would connect his engine to the muffler hung out my jeep window on one side a foot. When a lady wanted to raise chickens I was there with chicks. When Mr. Simpson fell from heat stroke, I delivered him to Mrs. Simpson. When Auntie Agnes died in Alabama, I delivered her ashes. I was sure she was leaking out on me all day.

Chapter Two

The Fright Attendant

The Beer Drinking Contest

Laughter filled the air as I sat at my dining room table eating pizza with my husband Terry, and the kids. We were celebrating the first Seahawks playoff win in history. The Seahawks were going to the Superbowl! We want to go to the Super Bowl. "Isn't there some contest you kids could enter to win free Super Bowl tickets?" I said and pondered if I had ever won a ticket to a sports game. And then it came back to me... I was standing shoulder to shoulder in the middle of twelve stuck-up 21 year-old girls in the Houston Sheraton Hotel bar. We had lived there for four weeks for flight attendant training and had four more weeks until graduation. At twenty-nine, I was considered a dinosaur by the younger girls and ignored by most as being too old and "Uncool." The radio announcer motioned for silence and said into the microphone, "And now, live from the Houston Intercontental Airport Sheraton, we have a dozen beautiful girls in stewardess training, drinking beer to try to win tickets to the Astrodome. The winner will sit in our press box for the live coverage as our Astros take on the Montreal Expos." I was not nervous at all at I summoned the spirits of my drunken German ancestors. "One, two, three, GO!" I tipped my bottle and my head back as far as it would go and let them meet happily. "Eight seconds!" We have a winner. I was the official fastest beer drinker in the contest. I just smiled at the catty little brats and stepped forward and claimed my two tickets. I said to the announcers. "Thank you, and see you at the game!"

Five Hundred Black People and Me

The tiny braid-covered heads slowly rose above the back of the pew in front of me. The girls couldn't have been more than four and six years old and their jaws dropped open at the sight of me. Their adorable astonished faces were highlighted by their wide inquisitive eyes. I had the distinct feeling they had never seen a white person. My flight attendant school friend Irving blended right in but as I gazed over the hundreds of well-groomed heads and fancy floral hats I noticed I was the only white person at church that morning. Irving and I had felt homesick after four weeks of living at the Houston Intercontinental Airport Sheraton Hotel and our handsome black doorman, Stacey, gave us directions to his church. We drove my hot red & black Camaro endlessly until we arrived at a large white church on the outskirts of Houston. Irving and I sang and prayed along with the flock and I noticed two adult choirs, a teen choir and a children's choir who were accompanied by an orchestra, blues band, rock band or brass band at various times. As the adult gospel choir revved up with the band, part of our swaying flock began to faint. Well-built nurses in white dresses drifted down the aisles with smelling salts and revived those slumped in the pews as the hymn reached a fever pitch I had never known. After an hour of singing and praying the minister began his sermon. He was of medium height and weight but the way he carried himself and spoke The Word of God began to bring down the house. Shouts of "Amen!" rang through the air and more fainting began. Filled with awe of the Spirit and with fear of damnation, I glanced at my watch and realized another hour had passed. I whispered to the lady next to me and asked her when the service ended and she replied, "We're just getting started. We break for lunch at two and begin again at four." We had a major exam the next morning so I tapped Irving's arm and pointed to my watch. He made a covert motion at the door and when we all jumped to our feet to sing, he and I slipped out the door. Driving back I wasn't sure which would be worse: Eternal damnation for ducking out of church early or getting kicked out of flight school.

Is This Your Pumpkin?

I was sitting with my eyes tightly closed, stiff-armed on my hands with my chin tucked down on my chest running the evacuation commands through my head over and over again, "Bend Over Heads Down! Come This Way! JUMP AND SLIDE!" I was as stiff as a board with fear. I'm not afraid to fly, I'm afraid to crash. Watching videos of every single commercial plane crash in history during training didn't help much either. Still, I survived training, went on to have a lady puke on my feet during my first flight and learned that I too get airsick during turbulence. Besides all that, it was pretty exciting to use my free flight benefits for the first time. I got my wings in April and was still on reserve in October and decided to go see my mom and dad in Malta, Montana. (Smallta, as mom called it.) I flew up to Billings and connected to a crop-duster to Wolf Point. Mom and dad were so excited to see me in my new uniform with my fake gold wings. And I was happy to see them too because it turns out I get home sick easily also. We had a grand old time visiting for four days and my mom gave me a big pumpkin she grew to put in the crew room for Halloween. The only snag is pumpkins are round and roll during take off. Betcha didn't know that. So the plane has took off and I start breathing again and looked down to where I had put the pumpkin under the empty aisle seat. It was gone. I craned my neck to look at the aft jump-seat and the male flight attendant was holding it on his lap. Oh man! I was so sure I'd get fired. A few minutes later I heard a voice say, "Oh miss, is this your pumpkin?" I weakly admitted to my crime and he said, "Well, you certainly woke us up. It's not every day a pumpkin comes hurtling down the aisle at us like a bowling ball!" I turned bright red and asked if I was going to get fired and he just started laughing. So, the moral of this story is: When flying with pumpkins, use the overheads. On landing, open them slowly.

Air Force Cadets

"Please direct your attention to the forward part of the cabin as your crew shows you the safety features on board our DC-9." The sea of scruffy-haired and shiny-eyed men ignored us. They were loud, rowdy, and laughing very hard. They had the energy of a herd of wild horses. United States Air Force Academy cadets. As I went down the aisle I smiled and said, "Would you like a beverage?" "Gimme a coke!" "I want 7 Up!" "Got any beer?" Eight weeks later, as the same group of airmen filed for vacation, in I pointed at the overhead bin and said, "Hat there, fold your blazer and put it there." I couldn't let these fine-looking airmen leave MY plane with wrinkled uniforms. A cadet looked at me and said, "Were you a TI ma'am?" After take-off I smiled and said, "Would you like a beverage?" "Yes ma'am!" Coke please Ma'am!" I laughed as the sea of shaved headed, atop straight-spined, polite airmen, all looked up at me. "Thank you maam!"

(I later learned that a TI is a training instructor or more commonly known in the army as a Drill Sergeant)

R & R Doughnuts

It had been a rough flight from New York to Fort Lauderdale the night before. Lots of turbulence and a lot of that weird dropping feeling on the plane like when an elevator drops fast. In between services I was on the back jumpseat with my head hung over my barfbag, just trying to survive. Once at the hotel I climbed in bed and curled up in a little ball waiting for the room to stop spinning. Yes, I did get airsick a lot as a flight attendant. I just didn't care. I wanted to see the world. The next morning, we were in the lobby at O'Dark Hundred in Fort Lauderdale and I had only slept a few hours. I felt like crap. On our way to the airport our first flight attendant, Christy, who was in charge, asked the van driver to stop at R & R Doughnuts. He pulled over and she turned to me and said, "Gretchen, it's your turn to help me carry the doughnuts." I was so sick and tired I could barely move, but I hauled my sorry self from the van and limped listlessly after her. I'm a team player unless dead. As I followed her through the door it seemed odd to me that it was nearly dark inside. I noticed the cigarette machine and choked on the smokey air. There were five young men sitting at the counter and the doughnut server had his back to us. Seemed odd he wasn't wearing a shirt. Christy shouted out, "We need the usual!" Well, it wasn't a man. It was a VERY topless young woman with huge bazookas holding a tray of doughnuts. I looked down at the floor and studied the peeling linoleum and took the box of doughnuts and tried to smile at her face without noticing her lack of uniform beyond a tiny G-string. I don't think she got the memo that modesty is a virtue. We got to the van and my face was very red. Christy couldn't stop laughing and the pilots joined in. My pal and buddy-bidder Theresa looked at me and said, "Um Gretch, you don't look so good." I probably didn't, but at least I had clothes on!

The Baked Baby Suit

"Oh miss" the young soldier said as I reached over his head to turn off his call button, "I seem to have a problem with my baby. She just threw up all over herself. "I looked down at the cute, chubby little girl and asked how old she was. "She is only six-months - old and I'm taking her to see my parents for the first time." Boston to LA is about five hours and we had just finished our meal service. I smiled warmly and said, "Don't worry about a thing, I'll help you put her in a clean outfit. "His dark eyebrows came together and I followed his gaze down to the tiny diaper bag. "I didn't bring another outfit." My brain spun wildly for a minute before I could think of what to do. Sure an FBI specialist for what to do in a hi-jacking trained me, but they seemed to have forgotten to train us about baby puke. "I have an idea. I can wash and dry her outfit in an hour and in the meantime you can roll her up in a blanket." I took the soiled outfit to the restroom and pumped as much soap as I could and then filled the sink with hot water. After a wash and rinse repeat cycle I was good to go. I did some serious wringing out and popped into my galley and decided on a hot start then a heat reduction, like a blackberry cobbler. The MD80 aft galley is a tiny hole off to one side of the rear aisle and I shut the curtain, lest the passengers saw what I was up to. After fifteen minutes at 425, I lowered the heat to 325 and rotated the suit every ten minutes. I was sliding out the narrow oven rack when my buddy-bidder Theresa showed up. She looked at the fuzzy terrycloth and said, "Whatcha makin' buddy?" I smiled at my fresh, dry little outfit and said, "Oh, just baked baby suit."

The Really Big Pinata or Odd Things People Bring on Planes

I was standing just inside the airplane doorway in Merida and tried not to let my jaw drop open. "That's a really BIG piñata." I said with what I hoped was a friendly smile since I was thinking, "What was she thinking?!" The young brunette held it higher and said, "Can you put this in the closet?" The main body was the size of a round laundry basket and the bright yellow points on the miniature sun stuck out all over making it roughly the size of a washing machine. Even the 747 didn't have a closet big enough for this bad boy, and we were on a little 737. I walked out into the jet-way and reached for the loops at the top and assured the young lady it would be safe, down in bin one. I zipped down the stairs and enjoyed the look on the rampys' faces as they admired what was possibly the biggest piñata ever made. And then there are odd things that are small when you see them, like tigers, which will someday be big enough to eat you. "Yes sir, let me show you to your seats and I'll get the seatbelt extension for your tiger." The little white and black Siberian tiger cub carrier was snugly belted in and I got to pet him after take off. "The captain is expecting you, please follow me." I said to the medical courier with a small Igloo cooler full of body parts. Couldn't help but wonder what was in there as I had coffee in the cockpit after we finished the service. "How on earth did you get through security with that plant?" I said to the teenager in the Grateful Dead tie-dyed tee shirt out of Missoula connecting to SFO. "When my roommates dropped me off at the airport they said it would be nice to give my aunt in Berkeley this little tomato plant for a hostess gift." Some room mates, sending a kid with a pot plant on a commercial flight! Our 737 landed in Houston and I gave the greeting over the PA, opened the door, and had the first class flight attendant say our good byes as I dashed down the stairs for the world's biggest piñata. I was holding it up for the nice lady as she came out the door. She was so happy. Nearly thirty years later I still wonder where that little sun ended up and more importantly, how much candy did it hold?

Chapter Three

The Temp/Sub/Reserve

The Stinkiest Place I Ever Ate Lunch

It was pretty exciting being promoted from the bulging to the dump-truck. Okay, it really wasn't so much a promotion as a rotation with everyone else, but as I looked up that orange City of Seattle engineering truck, it looked about two stories high and darn exciting. Not that I didn't like digging ditches out of the Haller Lake office. I certainly didn't have to count calories or do my Jane Fonda tape! I had to eat like a horse just to keep big enough for those long days of endless ditches. So after three months, I was finally assigned a dump-truck, with my buddy Debbie. We had both been recruited from the City of Seattle park department custodian pool, to the engineering department because in 1978, Seattle mayor, Wes Ulman,had been given the federal mandate to put women in traditional male jobs. The male jobs paid better than most of the secretarial jobs and many of us women were ready to get dirty for the big cash. When Debbie and I were assigned the same dump-truck, with driver Jim, we were delighted! We took turns riding shotgun and from way up high in that truck you could SEE EVERYTHING for miles and miles. Our week rotated daily with Monday and Tuesday being odd job days. We'd lean against the hallway each morning with our driver and the boss would hand him our orders and off we'd go! We could be picking up sod from the bull-gang ditch diggers, or filling in potholes or hauling brush to the transfer station...The transfer station! The Wallingford transfer station was a place we visited most days, but rarely got out of the truck. Jim would just back in and make the dump. But every Wednesday, we had a LONG garbage run that ended in Wallingford. We'd start in Ballard at 15NW and 85th NW and sweep all the sidewalks. Then we'd cruise down the hill to Golden Gardens park, to the flat section below the bluff. Debbie and I walked that entire meadow from the north to the south end with those long-handled garbage-spearing poles and trash sacks while Jim waited in the truck. Then we'd pick up all the trash, from the park restrooms, and do the shoulders around the Hiram H. Chittendon locks. It took about four hours. Then we'd hit the transfer station for lunch. Jim had twenty years at the City, so he always wanted to eat lunch with all his cronies. We'd climb down from our huge truck and follow him across the huge building and up the stairs. Now a transfer station is where all the garbage goes before it is loaded up in containers to be hauled out to the dumps, in outlying areas and they smell BAD. Debbie and I would follow him up a long staircase to the upper level where the lunchroom was located and sit along the tables with the garbage men. They were always excited to see us because we were the first women ever, hired for that job. We were strong and buff from months of work and Debbie and I were both genial people. We were a good crew for Jim because he was one of the most jovial people I have ever worked with in my entire life! Those garbage men were so friendly and funny, but boy did they smell bad. I mean really bad. Even inside the lunchroom with the door closed that lunchroom just reeked like garbage. It took us a few weeks to learn how to eat, and not smell at the same time. We looked forward to bullshitting with our new friends every Wednesday. It was the slinkiest place I ever ate lunch.

Pant Shopping Between Classes

I subbed a lot at Shorecrest High School in 2004. I had just finished my third period English class and decided to write my name higher up on the white board. I wasn't tall enough so I climbed up on a chair and wrote my name but then two things happened at once. I started falling off the chair and decided to jump down. As I was falling/jumping, my slacks caught the sharp metal corner of the eraser tray underneath the whiteboard. I felt a sharp pain on my backside and heard an ominous ripping sound. When I straightened up I felt my rear end and nearly fainted. My thin, thrift store navy pants had torn in a giant L shape that would have covered eighteen inches of tear, if measured horizontally. I got dizzy with fear. Teenagers thrive on hazing substitutes. It was late spring and hot outside and I didn't have so much as a sweater with me to tie around myself! I looked at the lesson plan and thanked God for giving me a one-hour planning time added to my thirty-minute lunch. The snag was, how to get from the room to my car. I grabbed my purse and locked the door. Unfortunately for me, I was on the back side of the building near the portables, as far from the front of the building as possible. I knew the students didn't look at old people and that no one would notice me if I was nonchalant. I stepped out of the room and waited for the bell to ring. Once the hall was flooded with hormonal teenagers bouncing around wildly, I crab-walked down the two long, sloping halls to the office. I told the secretary that I had a small problem and needed to leave the building for my lunch break. When she asked what my problem was I told her it was too embarrassing and she said, "It can't be that bad." I told her I had a small tear in my pants from jumping off a chair and she said she wanted to see it. She came around her podium and I rotated away from the wall, and she started howling with laughter and grabbed the office manager who joined in with her. I took that to mean I could leave the building but I knew I could not make it to Kenmore, and back, before the next class started. I ran backwards across the parking lot to my mini-van and raced to the Lake City Value Village. By then I didn't care if anyone saw me. I was around a size fourteen at the time, but didn't want to take any chances and grabbed the first size sixteen pants I saw and dashed in the dressing room. My blood pressure finally came down, as I zipped them up and tore off the tag and paid for them. Back safely in my classroom, I grabbed my copy of the attendance sheet, took a few deep breaths and looked forward to another dramatization of Shakespeare's 'Julius Caesar,' WITHOUT my behind on display.

The Accidental Milkshakes at Brookside Elementary

I stood before the sixth graders taking attendance, recognizing many names. When I finished a strapping-twelve-year old lad asked me, "Aren't you the sub who gave us milkshakes in kindergarten?" I looked closely at Jacob's face and as I did the strangest thing happened. His jawbone shrank and his face became round and his two front teeth were missing. I was now standing in front of the kindergarteners in the class of Liz Travis, giving sacks of sugar cones to her helpers to pass out to the rest of the class. I had just read the book, "Who Invented the Ice Cream Cone?" Liz had left ice cream in the freezer to celebrate the birthday of the ice cream cone. I called the first table group up front, opened the box, and to my horror it had melted. How could it melt in a half hour?! "Class, I'm afraid it has melted so we can't have ice cream cones." I announced. An uproar met my ears as the twenty-six students revolted against the skipping of ice cream cones. "One two, eyes on you!" I shouted. "One two three, eyes on ME!" Near silence with low grumbling ensued and I said, "We will have to suffer through MILKSHAKES!" A cheer went up and I carefully poured the blobs into the sugar cones, to the delight of the children. Seven years later, twelve year old Jacob's jawline stretched out and I could see his teeth had finally grown in and he held the promise of a teenager before too long. "Why, yes Jacob, that was me, I'd forgotten all about that."

The Wrong Pants

My pants slipped down a few inches again. I tugged at the waistband again. I knew I hadn't lost weight because I had been eating like a pig lately. I wasn't completely awake because it was only eight in the morning. I start working in my library every morning at seven but I wake up at nine. I can do several functions efficiently sleep-working, like setting up student folders and laying out nametags. I finished using the restroom, noticing that the waistband on these black slacks seemed wider than what I remembered. I put on my glasses, and looked at it. There were two thin yellow strips of some sort of non-skid cord running around it. I'd seen that before when I was doing laundry. Not MY laundry. I was wearing Troy's Safeway slacks! That explained everything. I hope no one noticed the girly-girl Gloria Vanderbilt embroidery on the back of what Troy must wearing at Safeway.

Chapter Four

Cruise Ship Jobs

If You Spanked My Spanx, You'd Break Your Hand

After I applied for a cruise ship job, I panicked about my figure or lack of thereof, and my interview was coming up fast. So Brenny and I dashed to Alderwood Mall Nordstrom's, for my first Spanx. I drove because you'd think she was from Ballard not Greenlake if you got in a car with her. I was so excited because I had heard my young friends in their forties talking about them! One thing men never know from experience is how fattening being a wife and mother is! It's totally brutal to see Terry and the kids eating 10,000 calories a day and never gaining weight. So we got to Nordstrom's and met the most wonderful saleslady in the world. Her name was Kathy Lauterbach. She was warm, friendly and very knowledgeable. Plus she didn't look like she was getting ready to dash off to a disco like some of the younger salesladies do. So I told her I wanted a Spanx and she knew (probably from looking at me) exactly what I needed! I was very excited until I tried on what she gave me. My Spanx could not cope and rolled right down my back! So Kathy brought me a shorter Spanx and if you spanked my Spanx you would have broken your hand! You could have flicked a quarter against my butt and had a twenty-foot rebound. Seriously.

Well it turns out that Spanx does not make a product quite generous enough for my well-rounded body and I felt so dejected. After pouring my copious self unsuccessfully into several Spanx, I appreciated Brenny not laughing at me. Luckily, Kathy knew right what to do! She told me that there was a product she used occasionally from a company that has been around forever that might be just right for me. And it was! She brought me a TC brand EVEN MORE pantie. And was it even more wonderful than anything I could hope for. So I bought that and call it my Spanx even though it's not because Spanx is such a cute name. Brenny looked so relieved that I was happy because she knows how much I want a cruise ship job. You have to look presentable when you are working with the public. She bought me lunch at the food court where I made a terrible pig of myself because I was armed with my Spanx-like product in my la-dee-da silver Nordstrom shopping bag with its sturdy twine handle. Bren naturally ordered the Japanese curried vegetable platter while I ordered everything they could deep fry in batter. Ummm, tempura. Yet permura on your booty. After lunch our crankiness subsided and we were ready for one more round of earring shopping. But that's another story.

Fear Factor

There are so many dangerous things on a cruise ship that it's not even funny. Below-deck stairs that are more like ladders. Water-tight doors that can squish you in half, and the biggest danger; my runaway imagination. With my claustrophobia, my fear of being assigned a cabin below the waterline is now out of control. That is my biggest fear. My smallest fear is getting a top bunk since I'm a Bladder Day Saint, a condition that nighttime does not abate. In between those fears is the fact that unlike my last ship job, our youth center does not close mid-day so I can take a nap. I'm now afraid I'll fall asleep at work, get thrown in the brig (yes, they do have them) get fired and get put off at the next port without airfare home. (Fact of ship life if fired) With our charge card over the limit, I'll have to hitchhike from Miami to Seattle or worse yet, I'll get put off at Stirrup Cay in the Bahamas and have to live my last twenty-four years there. Wait that might be a good thing!

Don't Touch My Washing Machine!

I am so fed up with my husband. I can't WAIT to go to work on the cruise ship! So, six months ago the dial on my old, rusty Maytag began to act up. I had to manually advance it through each cycle. Sounds easy right? That was for the first three months. Then the dial and machine had a fight and weren't talking to each other. It was like playing roulette to rinse the clothes. Then I'd pray to find a working spin cycle. So two months ago, Terry decides to "FIX" my washing machine. He snaked out the drain. Well, the drain wasn't broken! But he managed to prevent the machine from draining at all. Well, you know I am a bad wife. I've decided not to get it repaired before I fly out to work. I have been manually wringing out the wash for two months. I could probably beat Chuck Norris at arm-wrestling! Last week I was in my room and I could hear Terry spinning the dial on the washing machine. I yelled through the wall, "Don't touch the washing machine!" I ran to the laundry room and told him I had to add fabric softener. Like I have bothered with that in twenty-five years of marriage. When he drops me off at Sea Tac Saturday, I just KNOW he'll get all excited to be Mr. Mom. And then...He will try to wash clothes. And then... I'm a horrible person!

People are always surprised to find out how evil I can be.

Cabin Inspection on the MS Pride of America

When I saw, "Teach on a Cruise Ship" on the internet last year, I sat right up! I didn't know people took kids on cruises. They wouldn't if they had MY kids. So I popped out to Hawaii and worked on The Pride of America. We cruised ‘round and ‘round the Hawaiian islands and it was a blast. But cruise ships have a secret life. Below decks and behind passenger areas are narrow, mysterious hallways. They are all filled with the most interesting people you'd ever want to meet. I loved working on the top deck in Rascal's Kid Center. My coworkers were great, especially my supervisor, Goldfish. She had recently been promoted to supervisor from youth staff. The troubles began when they hired my roommate Jitterbug. She and I would get lost all over that ship because were forever trying to find short cuts to our cabin. Darn it if we didn't run into Goldfish half the time and try so hard to look un-lost. She would just roll her eyes and point us in the right direction. Sounds easy to find your way around on a cruise ship, right? Well, maybe for passengers that have signs and arrows! The Pride of America is four football fields long and fourteen decks high, not counting the engine decks. The Rascals Kid Center is aft deck twelve and our cabin was forward deck three. I lost ten pounds just getting coffee every morning. After eight weeks it was time to sign off from my temporary spring break job. Goldfish gave me a form to take around to the five department heads to turn in manuals, uniforms etc. The last thing on my list was: Cabin Inspection, Immediate Supervisor. I got to 3719 and my other roommate Robby was there. Her pal Brandon was there chatting with her. I told her Goldfish was on her way to inspect our cabin. Brandon got up to go and I took a good look at him. Movie star handsome and so buff that he made Will Smith look like little boy. I said to Robby, "We should hide Brandon in JB's bunk for inspection." Well, Robby, being the enthusiastic person that she is, grabbed the ball and ran with it. Not only did she want to prank Goldfish, she insisted Brandon strip down to his boxers! Now, I thought that might be going a bit too far, but I'm not known for my good sense so I went along with it. We had just gotten ready when Jitterbug came flying in the cabin shouting, "Goldfish is on her way! Look at this mess!" She ran to her bottom bunk and threw back the curtain and let out a blood-curdling scream that the captain could probably hear from the bridge and ran down the hall. Robby and I cracked up and when Jitterbug came back. She was so mad. Didn't stop her from yelling at Brandon, "Get back in there and be quiet!" Goldfish walked in the open door as the words left her mouth. I said, "Goldfish, Jitterbug is such a slob! Just look at her bunk, you should write her up." Goldfish leaned over and pulled back the lower curtain on the right of the bunk side and saw what I'm sure looked like a naked man. She stood up, looked at the three of us and said, without cracking a smile, "Cabin looks fine, Lollipop."

The Blue Kid on the Cruise Ship

I stared at the blue kid with dread. My blue slime was four times darker than the slime being poured by Scuba or Goldfish. My grandmother's voice rang soundly in the back of my head, "Haste makes waste." It wasn't so much that I'd been in a hurry making my slime for Slime Time Live on the pool deck as just plain excitement. I did pay attention as Goldfish showed me how to fill my bucket with water and add the cornstarch and blue food coloring; I just thought it would look cooler dark blue so I added a bit more. Well, the snag with food coloring is that it is easily absorbed into the skin. I knew that from a lifetime of dying Easter eggs in my sloppy, excited manner. What didn't occur to me was that I could potentially end up with a blue kid. Running poolside games with the other youth staff was one of the most exciting parts of my job. They had live music rocking oldies from my teen years and it was near-impossible not to dance. The Pride of America cruise ship job was the best job I ever had, except for the chronic seasickness. There was an hour at the start of every program where the kids had free time to choose from dozens of different games. I loved playing Candy Land with the tiny tots and Jenga or Uno with older kids, but nothing compared to those outside pool games! We ran all kinds of funny trivia games for families and the Slime Time Live was usually just two kid teams of four. We had already done the poopy diaper eating contest, which was really chocolate pudding in a Haggy eaten with their hands behind their backs; and we had done the trivia section with tri-boards. So the winners were standing in a small inflatable wading pool, and we were pouring blue slime over their heads as their parents snapped away with their cameras, and I was thinking my kid was far too blue! Thank God the kid and his parents thought it was funny and that after the poolside shower he was pale blue. I really liked that job and didn't want to get sent home before my contract ended in two weeks. When I got to work for the evening shift and took a good look at my kid, you could barely tell he was blue. He shouted, "Lollipop! Lollipop! Look at me! I'm blue!" I looked at him and so did my supervisor Goldfish. She just rolled her eyes.

Losing Weight With Noodle On Spy Day

I couldn't wait to get up to Rascals Kid Club for Mystery Morning! Of all the themed programs on the ship nothing could excite me more than pretending to be a spy. Ever since David McCallum captured my eight-year-old heart on the TV show, Man From U.N.C.L.E in 1964, I wanted to be a spy and go on missions with Napoleon Solo and Illya Kuryakin. So, now I got to. I met Noodle in the Rascal Room on deck 12 and we had six kids left behind for Port Play as their parents explored Kona and the surrounding area. Noodle, my fellow Washingtonian, from Spokane was what my grandmother used to call, "One long drink of water." At six-foot-four with bright blond hair and sparkling blues eyes he was adorable and had a fun-loving personality to boot. Noodle and I divided the work and I helped the kids make their "official" spy badges and write their spy code secret messages while he took the all the ransom notes and hid them all over the ship. When Noodle came back he "noticed" that some evil person had kidnapped Charlie the Seahorse. Now Charlie was a blue, much-loved over-sized vinyl covered stuffed rocking seahorse that lived in the padded toddler play area. Who could be so evil as to kidnap the most beloved toddler friend as Charlie?! Our spy team was going to solve the mystery, and with the two twelve-year-old boys finding the first ransom note, we were off to save Charlie! The snag for me was that Noodle had decided to depart from the standard search of ransom notes to "mix it up a bit." Noodle followed the oldest kids and I (Lollipop) brought up the caboose of six and eight year-old-kids as we searched the entire ship for clues. Ten clues that were spread the length of the 965 foot ship and up and down six decks, five times each. I don't normally need a calculator to write stories but we covered 4,825 feet and 50 staircases that morning. My favorite part of going through the ship as spies was that we had all kinds of secret codes to follow. Whenever we'd run into passengers in the hallways, we needed to be invisible so we'd do a Code Red, and crab walk stealthily against the walls and of course crossing the large reception area unseen necessitated Code Black or crouching down and tiptoeing silently. All good fun for when we finally got back to the Rascal Center and read the final note, which led us to the baby-diaper changing room where we "rescued" the "prisoner" Charlie. By the time we finished, the parents were waiting to pick up the kids for lunch. Most people on a cruise ship gain weight foraging through endless buffet lines, but I lost twenty pounds each contract and five that one Mystery Morning. Thanks Noodle!

Let Me Help You Back to The Passenger Area

I like to drink cold water. Really cold water. The stuff that comes off the Cascade mountains and into my glass at my kitchen sink. Yummy yummy. There was a big problem for me on the MS Jewel cruising from New York down to the Bahamas every week. Our refrigerator was broken in our cabin. No cold water. So after working my ten or twelve hours with the kids and my wild coworkers in the Splashdown Youth Center, I'd put on my nightgown, collapse in my bunk and want water. Cold water. I'm a spoiled cold water baby. Every single night, I'd climb back out of my bunk and throw my housecoat over my nightgown, put on my slippers, shuffle down the hall and around the corner to the drinking fountain. It was one of those huge refrigerated models and I LOVED that machine. I surprised the hell out of my Pilipino deck neighbors down there. My roommates and I were way down below the decks of most of the cruise staff with the cleaners and food workers and they just didn't get old white ladies down there. I was nearly three decades older than my coworkers and I forgot my nametag most nights. If I had a dime for every time I heard "Let Me Help You Back to the Passenger Area" I'd be a millionaire right now.

Dancing With Sponge Bob on the MS Jewel

As I entered the dim Spinnaker cocktail lounge I was assaulted by the noise of one thousand chattering kids. My friend Coconut smiled and waved at me and told me what to do. Our supervisor, Josh, was already down on the stage explaining to one thousand happy, half-drunk parents all about our complimentary child care center. Next thing I know, it's pitch black and the spotlight pops up on me at the top of the lounge and I hear Josh announce, "And all the way from Seattle, Washington, we have Ginger Snap!" The loud rock music started back up again and I smiled and waved at the crowd, danced my way down the carpeted stairs of the lounge and joined Coconut, Abracadabra and Nunchuk on the stage and started dancing with the rest of them. The crowd was going wild with the loud music and dancers on the stage and then everything went black and quiet and I heard Josh say, "And now, the moment you have been waiting for... SPONGE BOB SQUARE PANTS!" The stage lights came up and there was a deafening roar and out came a dancing Sponge Bob to the loud rock music. There were two of us youth staff dancing and waving and smiling on either side of Mr. Pants and you'd think Josh had introduced Mick Jagger and the Rolling Stones. Sponge Bob is the rock star for the under ten set for sure. The house lights came up and we scurried back up the stairs and back to our youth center as kids lined up to get their pictures taken by the ship photographer with Sponge Bob. I never did find out if Sponge Bob was Smile or Speedy!

Singing With Dexter on the MS Jewel

"How do you like working with the two to five-year old-group?" I could see the handwriting on the wall as my supervisor Martine asked me the question. The group I feared the most. Sticky, germy, cough in your face constantly: THE TODDLERS. Feared above all others and ready to infect me with global bacteria. "I hate that age group." I answered honestly. “OH well, that is what you are scheduled for" she answered with a smile. Turns out it I never stopped laughing those first two weeks until the infections robbed me of my laughter and replaced it with gut-wrenching coughs. But, before I got sick I had the time of my life. I went to the MS Jewel to meet people from all over the world and I did! Turns out that since most of the kids out of New York City were American, the toddler room curriculum was in English. Now, here is what cracked me up: All the American nursery rhymes have traditional melodies that I expected, BUT when sung by someone from Peru or the Philippines, the melody was often different. I would be helping a two-year-old putting on his shoes and hear all the songs I grew up with sung completely differently! It was like being in a audio-fun house where all the songs were off kilter. Mary Had a Little Lamb, Wheels on the Bus... Even the song "Dis is My Tinkerbonker" when sung by the

Canadian, Dexter, had an entirely different melody. As a former Cub Scout leader, I was trained to sing loud so the dozens of boys around a campfire could hear and join in here I was in the MS Jewel toddler room, and Dexter and I are standing shoulder-to-shoulder singing the Tinkerbonker song, at the top of our lungs, to two different melodies! The cute little kids were mimicking our movements and didn't even notice.

Chapter Five

Library Land

Odd People in Comfortable Shoes

I looked up smiling as the head librarian of Lake Washington School District gave an impassioned speech on the merits of the new Encyclopedia Britannica online database. Anne gave the comparative statistics as to why we should vote for the district to purchase this database over another database. Database, database, database. Favorite librarian topic I assumed as her best friend Mary began to argue with her. After nine years in the substitute pool and a grueling year at the University of Washington library graduate school, I had ARRIVED. I was sitting at the start of the year with the forty librarians from all over the district. I had a JOB. I listened intently as Anne and Mary's debate became more and more heated. Mary shouted at Anne, "You're so odd!" Then she burst out laughing. Anne tried to look dignified as she looked from the podium at her best friend of thirty years and replied, "You KNOW what they say about librarians?" She then smiled at her bestie and said, "They're odd people in comfortable shoes." I covertly peeked under the tables at all the shoes on all the feet, including my own. We were all wearing comfortable shoes.

The Christmas Party

I looked at Terry all cold and wet as I sat in my recliner in my PJs all toasty and said, "If you are too tired, we don't have to go." It was eight o'clock at night and he had just arrived home from delivering mail. "No Honey, I think it is important since you are still a little new, to go socialize with the teachers from Blackwell. Let me get my bathrobe. Now are you SURE it is a pajama party?" I assured him it was and we would have a super-fun time. As we wound our way to Ken's house, I peered out at the black, rainy night and said, "Gosh, I haven't been on this road since I delivered Dave Graham's route in 1983. It still looks exactly the same." It had been pajama day at Blackwell Elementary so I didn't need to change clothes after work. At lunchtime our secretary, Lisa, said everyone had to come to the party in their pajamas. Everyone at the table said it was a great idea.... We entered the party and I was excited to introduce my funny mailman to my delightful co-workers. Not one of the forty people enjoying drinks and food had on pajamas except Lisa. They ALL turned as one to look at the late arrivals and had the BIGGEST SMILES.

Camping in the Library

"No food in the library!" I said to Davyn as I saw him munching on a granola bar. "Look at this beautiful new carpeting and I don't want mice in my library." He put the granola bar away and I asked everyone to grab a corner of the tent to unfurl it. Dirt and needles and filth spilled from the tent and I realized my husband and son did not shake it out after their camping trip last month. So much for my beautiful new carpet. I looked on with horror inside as the two brothers next inserted the tent poles into each other creating a twenty foot long pole. Were the assembled poles ALWAYS that long?! I had the six kids ranging from six to twelve who were unable to go to camp with the rest of the school. After our writing lesson on evergreen trees, we were sitting on a small line of chairs next to the tiny ten foot square I had cleared from the boxes of books everywhere. While it was the fourth week of school, I still did not have shelves. My shelves arrived last week, but were the wrong size and were shipped back. The ten and twelve year old brother team had camped before and I had them showing the younger students how to assemble the poles. When the pole was twenty feet long it popped open a ceiling panel before I could jump up and guide it over sixteen feet of tables and boxes of books. I smiled and said, "Well done Davyn and Ben!" I next had, Joshua and Ming assemble the second pole with me guiding it so it didn't remove ceiling tiles. Smiling and praising the pole teams, I pretended this was part of my plan. I had no plan, or at best, a vague plan. It was now clear that the tent would NOT fit in the library. "Each team take the ends of the poles and we'll now carry them to the grassy area." The long poles barely cleared the tiny room and hallway, banging into all the new equipment still stored willy-nilly everywhere. Once we cleared the double doors I breathed a sigh of relief. The unscheduled sun had come out and the grassy area between our two remodeled buildings was dry. I directed Davyn and Ben to insert the twenty foot pole through the tent guides. The filthy tent flopped wildly and I pretended that was normal as the kids laughed. As we tried to insert the legs to the tent-bottom pins it occurred to me that it required strength. The three of us groaned from the exertion as we managed to insert the pole at both ends. We now had a half-circle of tent up flapping more crazily than before. Penelope, Joshua and Ming and I wrestled the second pole in place and the whole thing flopped over. What a disaster this lesson was so naturally I smiled and said, "Well done! All we have to do is tie the top of the tent to the crossed poles. "Now, it dawned on me that Terry and my sons are all over six feet tall and had ALWAYS done this for me. "New plan kids, everyone gently grab the bottom of the tent and pull it out to form a circle." The side that had been up in the air came down and amazingly enough it looked like a tent! "Time to go camping kids, everyone in the tent." I instructed the kids to sit down and they all protested, "It's too dirty Mrs. Nixon!" New plan... "Everyone close your eyes and pretend it is nighttime in the forest and listen for animal sounds." They obediently stood in the tent with their eyes closed except for Davyn who was running around on the grass. I let out a soft, "Who whooo." The kids giggled. Next we heard a huge "ROAR!" as Davyn ran at the tent like an attacking bear. Thankfully. "Okay kids! Time for some Bear Tag!" Everyone ran around screaming and laughing. It was all part of the unplanned plan.

Kindergarten Best Friends

I was walking down the school hall, at the end of my shift. I saw the two little girls and said, "Hello." The little black kindergarten girl was zipping up the little Mexican girl into a puffy coat and said, "I'm loaning Lupe my extra coat because hers doesn't have a hood. We are going to be friends when we are ninety-nine!" Lupe looked at her and said softly, "And in heaven after that."

Chapter Six

The Cranky Husband

Lake Serene, What a Nightgown!

The angry roar of the helicopter blades matched my mood as we approached Lake Serene. When we emerged from the forest towards the lake we could see the helicopter lifting a body-basket, and then it was gone. We looked down the steep cliff to the lake and wondered what had happened. Terry and I had just transitioned from health club friends and coworkers to dating. This was not a good start. He had picked out the Lake Serene hike from a hiking book published in 1975 and assured me it would be a snap. Maybe, if you are six foot three, two hundred pounds and used to gaining 2,000 feet in elevation in 2,000 feet of hiking. I had my little black skipper poodle Susie, as usual, and the "trail" ended up being a vertical ladder of wet, slimy roots. Terry carried Susie like a fluffy football under one arm and led the way. By the time we reached the top I was tired, hungry and thirsty. Terry said it was a short hike so we hadn't brought any food. After a half hour of hiking around the lake, trying to get cheered by the viewing the pristine beauty, I gave up and wanted to go home. The clouds were gathering black in the late afternoon sky, but didn't come close to my mood! We started back down which was way harder than going up. By the time I was on the logging road out I told Terry, "If you wanted to break up, you didn't have to try to kill me, you could JUST SAY SO!" I hiked ahead to the car and waited for him. I didn't speak a word to him for two months. When he did show up at my apartment with chocolate and flowers two months later, I caved in and we resumed dating. We laugh about it now thirty-five years later. That was in 1986 and the trail was closed for a long time and listed in hiking books, "Trail closed due to extreme danger."

A Canteen for my Birthday

I'd like to thank the inventors of flannel PJs, polarfleece pullovers and most importantly, GORTEX. When Terry bought me my Gortex jacket for Christmas in 1986, I didn't think it was very romantic. Forty years later it still keeps me dry! When you live near Seattle, Gortex is the Holy Grail of fashion. Today was the first cold, rainy day of what will be the norm here for the next nine months. I'm still shocked when people tell me they actually moved here from Southern California. I wouldn't live here in a million years if I hadn't been born here. Not the spot for a sun-loving girl. But with the right equipment, I've survived. Like when I turned thirty and opened my gift. All I could think was, "A canteen, how romantic." But you know what? That canteen saved my life one time. It was a hot August day and Troy, Teddy and I jumped in the van to pick up gear for scout camp and we got so thirsty! We were stuck at that horrible five-way stop in downtown Bothell forever. I reached down for my trusty canteen and realized that my husband is a saint. The patron saint of survival gear!

Painting the Gran Torino

I looked at the enormous hood skeptically. "That color doesn't look the same to me." I said to Terry, plus I realized one can of spray paint was not going to be nearly enough. He said it would match up when it had dried overnight so we walked the two blocks from our tiny studio apartment in downtown Bothell to Shucks Auto Parts. After we had another eight cans of paint we felt confident in our ability to not only remove the rust spots off the hood, but to create a paint job equal to the Sistine Chapel. Well, the next morning, I heard a voice in my head, which said, "Surprise! Surprise!" We now had a Gran Torino with ten shades of gold.

Mayoma Tu Tee-shirt Por Favor?

My face was bright red as I approached the first table in the Chitzanitza shopping plaza. "Mayomo Mi Tee-shirt Porfavor?" I said to the small lady. I held up my dollars and her face cracked into a huge smile. "When my husband drove over the speed bump the gas gauge showed a full tank of gas. You see it had only been stuck on E so we didn't need to use our money for gas so I can buy back all my souvenirs which I had returned for the money from you because that was the last of our cash, and we needed to get to the ferry." I don't think she knew what I said but the younger lady next to her did, especially when I repeated myself and pantomimed what had happened. Soon the one hundred ladies were rolling on the floor laughing as they rapidly repeated the story to the stalls next them and it went around the whole plaza. After a long drive from Tulum to the pyramid and exploration of Chitzanita, Terry and I had gone to the plaza and bought a hundred dollars' worth of tee-shirts, mini chacmools and onyx pyramids. Unfortunately, it was our LAST cash so when we got to the parking lot and Terry saw the gas tank empty he had a fit. We got out in the parking lot and were shouting at each other when the helpful policeman came by. Terry went on and on about how someone had siphoned off all our gas so he went for a gas can and put in enough to get us to the gas station a mile away. Then Terry backed out and went over a speed bump, which jarred the gas tank back to 3/4 full. He turned to me and pleadingly said, "Honey, can you please go back and buy all our souvenirs from the ladies?" I told him we could go together but he said he was too embarrassed. So, I swallowed my pride and went back and re-bought all our souvenirs, much to the delight of our Mexican vendors.

Run Terry Run!

We pulled into the wooded campsite and sat at our picnic table. We'd been all around Tofino and nearly drowned in the canoe the previous day. Seemed like a good day to relax. Terry said, "I can't believe how high the campsites are here in B.C. Sixteen dollars! It's only ten back home. I'll go pay the ranger and be back for lunch." I kept making sandwiches until he said, "I lost my wallet!" I was filled with dread and said. "All we have to do is retrace our steps." I thought about all the places we had gone in the morning with the last stop being the dump. We had sat on the hood of my old truck and watched the bears eating garbage for an hour. "Let's start at the dump. I'll drive." I hopped in my ancient white Ford 150 Supercab and drove through the pristine forest to the dump. We got out and started looking around but I had a bad feeling. "Honey, I'm tired. Can I rest on the truck while you look?" He nodded with his eyes glued to the ground. I sat on the hood of the truck enjoying the view when I saw the bear cubs ambling out from behind a rusty old van. I saw Terry lean down and pick up his wallet and that was when he noticed the two cubs. He froze for a second and then the mother bear walked out from behind the van. He started sprinting from about five blocks away. "Run Terry Run!" I yelled from the truck.

For a big guy, he can really move fast. He probably burned off a whole box of Pop Tarts with that sprint. He flew up to the hood of my truck and sat down panting. My blood pressure was still so high I was slightly dizzy. He held up his wallet and said, "Now I can pay for the campsite."

It's Too Heavy

I pulled my favorite sweater out of the dryer and stared at it with dismay. It had been shrunk down to a size zero. It wouldn't even fit my old baby doll Cathy. I ran up the stairs to the living room and held it in front of Terry's face. "Look at my sweater!" I yelled. He had a big smile and said, "I know. Isn't it great? I did the laundry." I sat on the end of the couch close to his recliner and explained about shrinkage. (Not that kind) I calmly told him I would prefer to do my own laundry from now on. I told him if he REALLY wanted to help he could push the vacuum cleaner around the house. His bushy cromagnum eyebrows came together and he frowned and said, "It's too heavy." My mouth began to drop open but I caught it. I placed my lips together and smiled and nodded. THIS coming from a man who hauls an 80 LB backpack. (Half of which is mine, much to my delight) AND who last week carried a 60 LB bag of kitty litter from Grocery Outlet across the road AND lifted my old 100 LB canoe to the top of my mini-van. (Much to my delight) I told him that I REALLY appreciated his help and then... I hired a cleaning lady.

That Wasn't Quite the Romantic Kiss I Was Thinking Of

Sunday night Terry and I were sitting in his dark man-cave watching the NBA All Star game, holding hands. It was slightly romantic. There were so many commercials that he was surfing to the next station so we could watch 'The Holiday' at the same time. There is one scene where that adorable Jude Law takes the equally adorable face of Cameron Diaz gently between his hands and says something mushy. Then he gives her that tender, "I'll cherish you forever" kiss. Only in Hollywood, I thought to myself. And in Harlequin Romance novels. The women in romance novels are forever getting their faces held. I thought about that a for few days and decided to test my theory. Last night as I was sitting in my warm, pink girl-cave, reading The Adventures of Sherlock Holmes, I could hear Terry come in from work. He was in the basement banging around by the wood stove a few minutes before he came to take his shower. I said, "Honey, could you please hold my face and give me a kiss like in the movies?" He walked over and leaned down and I saw with horror that his fingers were covered with black soot from the wood stove, but it was too late. He was giving me exactly what I asked for! His fingers were ice cold and stiff from work, covered with soot, and he curled his fingers like crab pincers and grabbed the bottom of my jawbones and gave me a little peck. I started laughing and couldn't stop. I should have known that the man that gave me Gortex clothing and camping gear for gifts wouldn't really study what Jude Law was doing with any degree of educational transference. It wasn't quite the Hollywood kiss I was thinking of.

The Accidental Vegetarian

Terry stared at the TV and recognized the hottest diet guru of 2015 on PBS, Dr. Joel Furman. "I'm going to kill you!" He shouted at the TV. Terry is not and will not ever be a vegetarian. Three years ago I was channel surfing and when I stopped on channel 9, an old guy with white hair was yelling, "Eat more! Eat more! Eat as much as you can!" I was automatically riveted to the screen and ordering his book on Amazon at the same time. I gained five pounds the first month. I went back and reread the book and found my error. You can have as much as you want of everything that tastes bad, but only one cup of anything yummy. Oops. After a few years of chewing my cud & swilling vegetable soup to keep my weight under five hundred pounds, I decided to try a recipe for vegepatties. After reworking three frying pans of goo I created a recipe I could live with. The eggplant parmesan recipe looked way too hard so I just made little towers of eggplant circles with the ragu etc. & threw some cheese on top. When Terry came home from work he asked what it was I told him it was lasagna, and he wolfed it right down & had seconds. He didn't even notice the meat missing. He was an accidental vegetarian.

When I Was Almost a Grizzly Bear Snack in Denali Park

The hair on the back of my neck stood on end. As I walked through the deserted campground, I could feel someone watching me through the trees. Odd that no birds were singing. Total silence. Where was everybody? It was like an eerie episode of the Twilight Zone. I gulped down my honey and butter sandwich, while I walked and looked down and said bad words to myself as I saw that honey had dripped all down the front of my shirt. I called out, "Terry! Terry!" and wondered where everyone was. The campground had been packed a few just a hours ago when we road the bus through the park enjoying the views of vast meadows, covered in wildflowers. Terry popped out of the bushes at me like he always does and I let out a small scream of fright. "Hurry Greta, we've gotta get out of here!" he said as he jogged past me in a most un-chivalrous manner, and headed towards the main road. I caught up to him and asked him what was going on. "The ranger said a hungry grizzly bear just came through and trashed the campground and they just finished moving the campers but they haven't found the bear yet." I raced past Terry with my sticky honey-covered shirt and yelled back, "Hurry up honey, I'm covered in honey!"

My Husband Thinks He's Jon Claude Van Dam

I waved at the young clerk at Canyon Park Big 5. "Could you help me find a basketball which fits my small hand?" I asked. He led me to the back wall and showed me the different balls for women. I had a moment of fright when I saw the official ball which had a price tag of seventy dollars. Even WITH Terry buying, that was too steep. I found a nice thirty dollar model and went to find Terry. He was with a young salesman, practicing kicking at this hanging sack of sand. He told the clerk he wanted to hang it out in the yard but the clerk told him it would fall apart in the rain. I approached and asked him what he was buying. He told me he wanted to practice kickboxing. I smiled as I remembered entering his man-cave the previous night. One of his cable channels was playing a Jan Claude Van Dam series of movies for hours and hours on end. He had been so engrossed that he did not know I was there. Or like most husbands, he did but ignored me. I smiled at my giant, hairy husband of about two hundred and sixty pounds and thought to myself, "My husband thinks he's Jan Claude Van Dam."

My Husband Will Buy Anything

I wish I could put a block on the infomerical channels. After Terry watches the Amish stove infomercial for four hours on television he'll ALWAYS buy another one. You could dress up as an old Amish guy and sell Terry anything. We have six Amish stoves and counting. When the boxes arrive, he spends an hour admiring the photograph of the old bearded guy driving his horse drawn cart full of stoves. I think that's why he married me. I sound Amish. One time thirty years ago I was working a flight and a man asked me if I was Amish because of my accent. Anytime I want to go out to dinner all I have to do is use my Amish accent and Terry is out the door. Now if I could only find an infomercial of the old, bearded Amish guy selling one of those robot vacuum cleaners!

Don't Embarrass Troy!

We were in the van, on our way home from Canyon Park Goutback Steakhouse. Contrary to my New Year's resolution to lose ten pounds, I was craving gout food. Terry told me not to embarrass Troy when we arrived at Kenmore Dollar Tree for coconut water, since he had only worked there a few weeks. He got out of the van and walked to the window, and told me to peer in the window at our son working. We had our faces on either side of the round window decal advertising all the hot sale items. So I did, and he starts tapping on the glass until Troy saw us. Then he flattens his nose up against the glass. I was thinking, "In what world would this NOT embarrass our child?" But I didn't say anything... just peered in as instructed...

Cougar Snacks are the Meatiest Ones

"See that moss hanging down honey?" I starred at the trees engulfing either side of the damp trail. "That's the kind I want to grow at home but it looks exactly what we have at home only it drapes down like that." I stopped and turned around to look at my husband. As usual his expression was blank because he hadn't heard a word I said. Nothing new there. So I continued my slow pace down the winding trail and admired the moss hanging down from the trees. I admired the thick moss covering the downed logs all along the sides of the trail with their baby hemlocks and huckleberry bushes popping out occasionally. I admired the moss under my feet and wondered if the person who invented olive green shag carpeting had hiked through the Olympic National Park rainforest. "Oh look Terry, there's a trail going down to the creek. Let's go down there." I started down the steep deer trail, careful not to fall or twist an ankle. Half walking and half sliding and clinging to a wimpy tree branch, I landed on the flat, muddy ground and looked at the tiny brook that I needed to leap over to get to the pebbly beach. I backed up, ran, and leaped to the other side and then turned around to watch Terry. He annoyingly took one big step to come up next to me. "Pretty." He said. We walked a dozen feet to a nice big mossy log and sat down side by side and listened to the sounds of the swirling water and birds singing. It was early afternoon and the sun played through the trees along the under-forest and dirt and pebbles and finally sand. I looked at the sand beneath my feet and noticed all the deer prints. My hand slid over to Terry's thigh and I thought maybe a kiss would be nice. Just as I was gathering steam for some romance he answered me. "Not that one. That's a cougar track." I dimly remembered the handwritten sign that I had seen taped to the front of the sign in desk at Kalaloch Lodge that said "Cougar sighted 6/8." I stared down at the print that looked exactly like it was made by the paws of Troy's cat Cloudy. Only about a hundred times bigger. I got up abruptly and said, "Let's go." I was so grateful for Terry. I knew for certain that cougars snack on the meatiest ones first.

Mail Theft Hurts Nursing Mothers

I was sunk back into my little green recliner on my heating pad feeling content after a lovely dinner of eggplant towers over vegeburgers. I heard Terry come in the basement door and hollered a greeting and waited for him to come upstairs. Five minutes later he plopped down in his recliner and said, "The strangest thing happened on my mail route today. You won't believe it."I was thinking after my own ten years of odd happenings and his thirty years of odd happenings on mail routes, that I had heard it all. Boy was I wrong. "Last month I was training a new carrier and when he saw the outgoing mail in a small box he got all excited. He said his wife ordered these special lactation cookies from the lady on my route." I had never heard of lactation cookies so I asked how his customer got beer into cookies. "I don't know what's in them but that's not the strange part of the story. The police were there when I pulled up and the lady ran over to me and told me that ten minutes before I arrived she saw a man in a hoodie steal her outgoing box of lactation cookies from her mailbox. What do you think of that Hon?" He asked. I thought about how horrible it was to steal from a new mother having lactation troubles and what I thought the worst thing that thief deserved. "I hope he eats that whole box and starts lactating."

The Christmas Tree Date

For twenty-eight years Terry and I picked out our Christmas trees together. Last year I looked out the kitchen window and saw a Christmas tree on the porch. I was crushed he bought a tree without me. I thought maybe he didn't love me anymore. I told him I felt sad we didn't go together. This Tuesday he came back from Grocery Outlet and told me the trees were in and he had seen one he liked. This morning we went to the store and I glanced at the trees, removed the tag, and went to pay for it as he loaded it in the van. While we were driving home he turned me and said, "Honey, you just picked out the same tree I liked best on Tuesday."

Chapter Seven

Babies, Kids and Teenagers

This Baby Did NOT Come With Very Good Directions

I had read all the 'What to Expect When You're Expecting' books over and over and over again including 'What to Expect the First Year' and none of them mentioned the situation I was in. Troy was two months old and I was rocking him in the big gold chair and all of a sudden his eyeballs started rolling back in his head! I called 911, in a panic and told the lady his eyeballs were rolling back in his head. She asked me all these questions and after a few minutes she asked what he was doing now. I looked down and he was asleep and told her so. Do you know what she told me? She told me babies' eyes roll back in their heads when they're falling asleep! I was so embarrassed. Troy was sound asleep and I couldn't help but thinking that despite all the books that I had read about babies that my baby did not come with very good directions.

Is This Your First Baby?

When Troy was five months old, I carried him all around the house. When you wait until you are thirty-seven to have your first baby, you carry them everywhere and never let anyone touch them. Around five PM one night, I was sitting on my bed playing with my baby. Terry came home from work and walked in the room. Troy saw his daddy, and flew towards him off the bed like he got shot out of a cannon! I wasn't fast enough to grab him and he fell on his head on the floor. He started screaming so loud, that I ran and called 911 while Terry sat on the bed and held him. I ran out to the road to bring the paramedics in. They came down the stairs and into the room and examined our baby. After a thorough exam the fire fighter asked me, "Is this your first baby?" Through heavy tears, I told him he was. Then he informed me that my baby was fine and that whenever they fall, they cry. I still feel bad about that. I feel bad about a lot of things as a mother. I did my best and Troy is a fantastic person, and the moral of this story is: Babies cry all the time, so if you are a new mother, try not to worry too much.

Come Back Troy!

Terry and I sat on the picnic blanket snacking, while my mom sat across from us chain-smoking and smiling while my step-dad, Lyle, bounced toddler Teddy on his knee. Troy was walking around near us looking at sticks and rocks on the ground. Someone yelled, "Foot races ages four through ten!" Terry and I got up and I took Troy's tiny four year old hand and said, "It's your turn to run honey." He lined up on the dirt line with the dozen other kids as the goal of running to and around the big maple tree and back was explained. Marymoor is a huge flat park, and the third week of July it is packed with company picnics like ours. The NALC picnic attracts hundreds of letter carriers and their families every summer. I heard the lady shout, "One, two, three, GO!" and watched as the kids took off running, got to the huge maple tree, circled it and start running back. I did NOT see my tow-headed mini-Terry coming back. I frantically shouted, "Troy! Come back!" The two dozen adults all started shouting, "Come Back Troy!" I began running with terror towards the tree. Two blocks past the tree I spotted him running towards the next company picnic. It was about a mile from our picnic. I got closer and saw dozens and dozens of white tents and a huge MICROSOFT banner and swarms of people milling around. I shouted, "Troy! Troy Troy!" A smiling lady came around the edge a the tent holding his hand and said, "Is this your little boy?" "He is so friendly and cute." Relief flooded me as I scooped him up and hugged him and carried him back towards the picnic. He looked up and said, "I wanna walk mommy." "I'm a big boy now."

NOT the Potty Teddy!

The tiny hand tugged on mine, and I looked down with horror, at my toddler. "Not the potty, Teddy!" While coffee cans of sand are wonderful for cigarette butts, they look surprisingly like potty chairs to the under three gang. Unfortunately we had just finished dinner at the delightful Kenmore Mazatlan restaurant and my curly-topped child was squatting over the top of the coffee can. The nice staff between Stupid Prices and the Idol Dry Cleaners had added the butt can, to keep Kenmore beautiful but I doubt Teddy's butt was part of the plan.

Lunch with Troy at Clifford's

The waitress smiled at me, and I ordered a French dip sandwich. Troy was dressed in a dress shirt, slacks and sports coat, with his blond hair neatly combed. At seven, he had grown his big front teeth. His second grade teacher, Jan Otiose, had assigned the kids to talk to someone for their community social studies unit who had a career they would be interested in. Troy wanted to be a chef, so we went to the cliff side restaurant with panoramic view of Lake Washington in our town. The float planes of Kenmore Air Harbor entertained us with their take offs and landings on the gorgeous sunny May day. "And what can I get for you young man?" The waitress asked. Troy looked up from his menu and asked, "Does the open-face baby shrimp sandwich mean they will be looking at me?

Teddy's Driving Lessons

I owe my ability to give Teddy driving lessons to my hairdresser, Janet Ferris. There is no way I could cope with that amount of white hair from fright on my own and I wouldn't try. How a kid gets to fifteen so fast is beyond me. I must have blacked out all of Troy's driving lessons three years ago because I don't remember a thing except for feeling like a bobblehead doll and at the stop sign at the end of our road. So, six weeks ago, I took Teddy to get his permit. Of course neither of us had read the small print that we needed his original birth certificate! We got the permit without it but no photograph but that was okay. He is bald as a billiard ball since he ended up with a "hot chick" hair cutter at Kenmore Great Clips and must have wanted to prolong the experience. So, we got the permit and I drove him in my green minivan to the Park and Ride lot behind St. Vinny's in downtown Kookmore. I hadn't seen him look that nervous since his 7th grade choir concert at KJH when he looked like he was going to be sick the entire show. He got out of the van and did a safety check. Then he got inside and did all the pre-drive checks. He started the engine and slowly crept down the slope, to the stop sign. That was when I noticed I had stopped breathing and I gave a big whoosh as I started again. He circled around and up the slope and shutdown the van to begin again. Again, and again and again. On his third start up, Kenmore sheriff chief Sether pulled up on the side of the lot and was having lunch. Beads of sweat popped out on Theodore's forehead as he slowly drove down the slope, past the chief. I smiled and waved and he hunkered down for some lunchtime entertainment. He had a big smile and I imagined he had given his kids driving lessons. Poor Teddy. He did not expect an audience, but he bravely made loop after loop, practicing his steering and parking skills. Over the last six weeks, we have been on roads and the highway a few times. I love the gap between when they get their permit and license and I get to be chauffeured all around town. Of course I trained him early on how to drive to the most important destination. The McDonald's drive-thru so I can get a cup of really good Seattle’s Best, coffee.

My Son the Sign Flipper

"Mom, can I have a cell phone? All my friends have cell phones." "Sure you can have a cell phone. Get a job!" I cruised over the hills of Canyon Park with the scent of McDonald's filling my mini-van. Double cheeseburgers, French fries, hot cocoa. All the treats that a teenager loves. It was March, bitter cold and the snow had started coming down in giant, icy flakes. As I came over the rise and climbed the next hill, I was excited to see my first-born child at his job. My son, the sign-flipper. At sixteen, this was his first job outside of yard work and house work AND he wanted a cell phone. So him having a real job was a big deal in our family. I reflected on the years of fun family life as I drove along. Holidays, family camping trips and vacations. Picnics in the swamp, making pies together. At eleven, he began that natural pulling away that a son starts with his mother. At fourteen, I couldn't stand being in the same room with him most of the time and at fifteen he was worse. At sixteen, I could feel him come back to me occasionally like we were pulling some familial rubber band. Short glimpses into the future. But I knew I would never be the rock star again. The days of being stuck together like glue were long gone. As I pulled up to where Troy was twirling his sign I could see his expression of consternation with me. I just wanted to give him hot food and drinks, while he stood in an inch of snow. I wanted to be his rock star, one last time. I lowered the window and he came over to accept my maternal offerings of food and love. "Hurry up mom! There have been hot chicks driving by waving at me!" No thanks, no gratitude, no manners. Hot chicks?! I drove off hurt, but full of pride, as I looked in my rear view mirror at my son, the sign flipper.

There's Someone Sleeping in my Chair!

Oh! My chair moved. I just sat on another teenager. Where do they all come from anyway? I guess I should turn up the lights before I sit down with my coffee. I felt like the mama bear in Goldilocks. After I found someone sleeping in my chair I went to sit on my couch. But there was another one there. Friends of Troy. I'm glad he is popular and all that but this is ridiculous. I can't wait to hear all about his adventure at the homecoming dance. When he put on his black Nikes with his tuxedo last night to leave I nearly died! I begged and pleaded with him to put on his dress shoes. I hope he didn't make his date cry. The apple didn't fall far from the tree with Troy. His dad's idea of dressing up is a forest green t-shirt without a hole in the arm pit. Terry has twenty-four tee-shirts. All forest green. He will wear his dress shoes to weddings and funerals so Troy didn't get much fashion role-modeling there. If I had a daughter, I could get the homecoming dance story retold for four hours with pots of coffee and tea and all the details. As it is, when the lumps get out of my chair and off my couch, I'll get a few grunts.

Beware of Boys with La-Z-Boy Chairs

I was driving down 73rd, towards the highway from work last spring and glanced over at St. Vincent DePaul thrift store. It looked like two boys carrying a huge chair down the sidewalk and I smiled to myself thinking, "That's something Troy would do." Then I looked again and realized it was my son Troy! He and his friend Devin had found an enormous Lazy-Boy recliner that someone had ditched in front of the store. He spotted me in the mini-van and started yelling, "Mom! Wait! Bring the van! MOOOOOM!" I panicked and the light turned green. They started chasing me with the chair. I stepped on the gas and flew home. Close one. They showed up a half hour later chair-less, and furious at me, for not stopping to give the chair a ride home.

Not My Pewter Ladle!

Having two teenage sons has desensitized me to household damage, to some extent. Especially when they have their friends over. For each teenager, the damage is exponential, not additional. I'm not sure why that is, but I know it to be a fact. I have tried to detach emotionally from all my possessions, for this reason. I'd need the whole world wide web to list all the things my kids and their friends have demolished around here. Usually I just accept it and figure someday they'll have jobs and they can replace the walls, floors, furniture and items that have been damaged. But this was different. As I looked in the kitchen garbage can, there was my pewter ladle. It was a wedding present from my Auntie Lois. Troy's friend Devin had used it for an ice cream scoop! Does a ladle REALLY look like an ice cream scoop? I guess it did to him. I took the pieces to the living room and held it up to the circle of teens busily killing zombies, on their video game and asked who had broken it. Devin had the good manners to admit his crime, and apologize. It's nice to have at least one Eddie Haskell in the house.

Walking Around with an Eighty Pound TV

Well, that was something different. Surprising the sheriff didn't turn up at my door! Teddy went to a birthday party Saturday night, and came back about eleven, and yelled down the stairs, "Mom, I got invited to sleep over and came back for pajamas." Well, that triggered my Mom-dar. He hasn't worn pajamas since he was twelve. So I go back to reading my latest trashy Jackie Collins novel, and at eleven-thirty I hear Teddy yelling, "Mom! Mom! I'm back!" I race upstairs and he's covered with sweat, and I asked him what had happened. Apparently, his friend Mikey convinced him that their friend Michael's party would be so much better with a second TV. That way, more of them could play video games together. Teddy and Mikey came and picked up Teddy's "pajamas" (AKA OUR TV) while I was downstairs reading, only to have dad Jon say, "NO." Only Mikey wouldn't help with the return trip, which left Teddy carrying an eighty pound television ten blocks, through downtown Kenmore! I'm lucky the sheriff didn't notice him.

Thor the Bunny

I sat staring down at the yard with my coffee in one hand, and clutching Milo my cat in the other. It wasn't quite light yet, but I could tell it would be a clear day. Ahhh, there he was. I could just barely make out Thor's light brown coat as he hopped through the open gate down at the bottom of our back yard. My he has grown in the last two years. Two summers ago, a strange car pulled into the driveway and Troy got out with his longboard in one hand and a cardboard vet box in the other. He shouted up at me, "MOM!" I went down to the driveway and he said, "We were long-boarding on the bike trail at Lake Forest Park by that big intersection and this bunny ran out and got hit by a bike and landed in the road. Everyone stopped and a lady yelled at us to grab the bunny and get in her car. She took us to the vet and the vet said the bunny was knocked unconscious but was okay. The lady just dropped us all off." Troy, Daniel and Devin and I walked into the back yard and opened the box. Troy said, "I want to call him Thor." I went and got a tiny bowl of water and told the kids the best thing to do was let Thor sleep it off. We laid him on a towel and turned the box upside-down over him and hoped for the best. The next morning when we lifted off the box, Thor stared at us, then started exploring our yard. He hopped down into the park but has returned every dusk and dawn, hence my creation of The Bunny Room. When the kids moved out we saved the upstairs room overlooking the yard for a guest room. So now, every morning I grab kitty and hot joe and watch Thor have breakfast. When it gets light enough he'll jump straight up in the air about two feet then hop out of the yard, his little cotton tail bouncing behind him.

Owen, Please Put Down My Bras

I was just finishing my laundry and had a few things in one hand and tossed it in the box I was carrying, for a temporary stop, to unload other things. I could hear my roommate coming in and said, "Look Owen, when I was at Safeway, Dakota gave me a banana box for your tools. It is nice and roomy for your new circular saw, and all the tools you and Teddy picked up this week." He walked over and looked at the big flat-bottomed box and looked inside. He scooped out the contents and said, "Wow, it even has some great rags in it. "I looked at the fabric in his hand and said, "Owen, please put down my bras."

The Sky Is Falling!

I sauntered down our gently sloping backyard with some blueberries for my quail thinking, "Quails! They're just like us!" "They love blueberries." Right as I reached the middle of the yard something flew straight out of the sky about two feet from my face. I looked up and something else was flying out of the sky! "HELP! HELP!" HELP!" "Ahhhhh!" I shouted. Then I looked down at the hard plastic frisbee golf discs at my feet and shouted, "STOP! STOP!" "I'm in the yard! Where are you?!" Next thing I know Troy's blond head pops up behind the raspberry patch and he says casually, "You okay Mom?" "Where in the heck are you kids throwing from?" I asked in a disgruntled fashion. "We go on the other side of the garage, and throw straight up and over it to the target in the middle of the yard." Our garage is two stories high. It is not see-through. At least on Mother's Day when I was working on my quail pen, Troy walked over, and handed me a bike helmet as he and his five friends played the course.

Teddy's Grand Canyon

I was all blissed out from a perfect day which included sunshine (not a given in Seattle) a last minute Seahawk win and a delicious pot roast dinner. Terry was even willing to sit in a chair next to the quail pen to keep me company As I cleaned the pen. I looked over and RIGHT NEXT to the trail under the pink tree at the foot of our yard is a 100 square foot pit, four feet deep, ten by ten feet. Teddy had dug out the dirt and hauled it to his and Owen's raised garden which they finished this morning. Someone would kill themselves falling in that hole. I was too tired from the Seahawk win to muster much yelling, and ended up with only a limp, "WHAT WERE YOU THINKING?!" Plus I yelled that they had dug up my quail cemetery. To which Owen replied, "Excellent. That will make great fertilizer."

Chapter Eight

Cub Sprouts

Beware of Boys with Knives

Beads of sweat popped out on my brow as my ten Bear Cubs laid their brand new pocketknives on the tables in front of them. The moment every den mother dreads had finally arrived: The third grade carving unit. I was feeling slightly dizzy and faint at the bloodthirsty expressions on their little faces and wondering what had happened to my innocent little tiger cubs. There was not a trace of that toothless, round-faced, babyish look about these potential killers. And that was what scouting was all about wasn't it? Trying to civilize these little demons into law-abiding productive citizens, right? The boys shifted from foot to foot impatiently, surreptitiously grinning at each other like they we ready for starring roles in "Lord of the Flies." Geez, I was so worried, that I could feel my blood pressure rising by the second. And why on earth did Carlos have buck knife?! I watched the boys finish the cub scout promise and I introduced the unit. I stared with gratitude into the eyes of the moms and dads that stood stoically next to each boy. With my pockets full of bandages, I passed out the bars of Ivory soap that I had traced bears on and mumbled a prayer for no injuries. And there were NO INJURIES! The boys were delighted with their tiny bears and it was fun to see how different they all looked. I could predict which bears would be carved in

3D and I knew Troy's would not be one of them, but I smiled knowing that there would be some clean boys at Kenmore Elementary the next day.

Cub Scouts with Beer Bottles

"Okay boys, today is Earth Day so we are going to carefully cross the street with our buddies and pick up litter in the park." It was like a demented Easter egg hunt with the little boys running around the woods hunting down nasty old beer and wine bottles and showing them to me. Two hours later the bottom of my navy den mother pants were soaked with stale beer and slug slime. Who knew slugs LOVED beer so much? "Look Mrs. Nixon! This wine bottle is half full!" Alex charged at me and I tried to escape but failed. His jumping up and down motion efficiently coated me with a new fragrance. Ewww, Eua De Vino or was that spit? AND it has a thick, sticky quality. No. Please God no. Fermented slug juice. Ugh.

That Was the Best Slug I Ever Ate

The flames from the bonfire seemed to lick the black sky with only the outlines of the huge fir trees illuminated. I had never seen such a huge campfire and was slightly worried one of the smaller boys might fall into it. Camp Brinkley. After a long year of organizing units to move the boys along in their scout ranks, it was my time to relax. The dads took over at camp and spoiled me rotten. Every morning I could hear them yelling at the kids to get them up, dressed and organized for meals at the longhouse. I just laid in my toasty sleeping bag on my deluxe Fred Meyer's cot, and gazed dreamily at the canvas ceiling of the platform tent. Our first year there together was particularly fun because our boys were only seven that year. Joe and Clark had found out that we had one of the only resident scout camps for the little boys and asked me if I wanted to go. I had been leading day camp for pack 622 for five years by then with Troy and it sounded so much more fun! With my dark green mini-van full of cubs driving out of Monroe, I had managed to get lost and we were hours late to check in. I was in awe of the beauty of the camp, nestled into an old-growth forest, with a tiny, pristine lake in a picturesque meadow. We found the sign-in area, got our gear into the carts and our camp guide, an older boy scout led us to our campsite. Teddy and my group were greeted by the other twenty boys and dads with much yelling and hullabaloo. "Mrs. Nixon!" The little boys yelled at me, "We found you a secret campsite!" I followed my dear little den fellows about fifty yards from the rest of the campsite, up a tiny hill overgrown with salmon berry bushes to my hidden platform tent. All the boys were in a "first time at overnight camp" frenzy and since both sides of my tent were tied open, they raced through and around my tent at breakneck speed. All I could do was laugh and relax. I had had to be the bad guy a few times and scold them during the year to get them to settle down enough to pass their advancement requirements, so it was blissful to just enjoy them. After an hour of running through my tent, the boys discovered an enormous stump on the hillside just past my tent. It instantly became a huge sailing ship complete with a brig down in the underside cave formed when the tree fell over and the roots exposed it. Oh the fun of camp: knives, guns, bows and arrows, arts, crafts and swimming and boating in our private lake. And NO COOKING! Three times a day we'd march to the long house for meals and I'd endure the shouting as the lines of 200 boys and dads did their competition for the loudest group of campers. The loudest ate first. But at night, the real magic of camp began. We'd round up our troop and fish around for flashlights and hike to another pack's campsite for friendship fire. I sat in my low-slung canvas chair back a bit from the fire as the songs and skits and snacks commenced. Our hosts offering to us was slugs on a stick. They were made from the biscuit dough in those little metal tubes and wrapped around toasting sticks. "That was the best slug I ever ate!" I exclaimed to the tiny red-haired tiger cub from the other pack. I knew exactly what I was doing. As soon as one of my ten wolf cubs heard that, the competition between the scouts began. I must have eaten twenty slugs, fifteen s'mores and washed it down with a gallon of apple juice. The competition was fierce to garner the praise of the only mom brave enough to join them at camp.

Chapter Nine

Health and Beauty

My Exercise Pants Made Me Fat!

The elastic waistband. Number one enemy for those of us chronically losing the Battle of the Bulge. When Terry gifted me with my first pair of sweat pants in 1987, I remembered thinking,"Ew, purple. That's what my MOM and OLD LADIES wear." But, they were OH SO COMFORTABLE. If you want to lose weight seriously, you have to pitch any pants with ELASTIC WAISTBANDS. Not like I'm going to do that but I'm great at telling OTHER people what to do. Here are the other enemies of those of us losing the Battle of the Bulge:

2. Food that tastes good
3. La-Z-Boy chairs
4. La-Z-Boy Chairs with heating pads
5. Books
6. Cars
7. Any home made food, especially cookies
8. Beds (When you're over sixty)

9. Jane Fonda exercise videos, because after five minutes you THINK you've burned off 10,000 calories and get to eat that much.

10. Overactive taste buds (my sister Pam's theory)

How My Tom's Deodorant Made Me Gain Five Pounds

Last month after Brenny and I shopped for unmentionables, we stopped at Kenmore Super Supplements so she could pick up some stuff. I was looking for deodorant made with natural ingredients. Well, Brenny told me she liked Tom's. I'm picky about smells so I smelled several until I found peach. It smelled like a juicy peach and I got pretty excited but trouble started the next day. After I put on my new peach deodorant I did my Jane Fonda exercise tape and the next thing you know, I smelled like a giant peach pie baking! I went crazy when I smelled that smell! I craved grilled cheeseburgers, potato salad corn on the cob, watermelon and WARM PEACH PIE WITH VANILLA ICE CREAM! So we had to have that for dinner a few days. The next thing you know I had gained five pounds. Yikes. Lucky for me, Tom's deodorant comes in a very tiny amount for a very high price. Way out of my league. So I'm back to my cheap Suave Ocean Fresh deodorant, which smells unfoodlike and costs half as much.

The Walking Man on the Bike Trail and Other Indignities

After blasting down the bike trail a quarter mile, I was winded and stepped to the side to catch my breath. I heard soft footfalls next to me and watched the tall man walk past. As I rested I visualized myself roaring past him at my top speed. It just didn't work out for me. My blazing fast top speed jogging is so slow, that not only did I not roar past him, and I could not catch up to him. Of course he had legs as long as Gulliver and a stride a mile wide. Every morning after that I waited for The Walking Man to get a really good head start past my house to avoid the humiliation of getting passed up while jogging by a walker. Tough on the ego that was.BUT, not as bad as the new mother pushing a stroller whizzing by me.

Chapter Ten

Friends

JoAnn and the Marshmallow Sticks

"Um, JoAnn, how far is the tent from your face?" I said. "About six inches I'd say." JoAnn said. This was not the highlight of our girl's camping trip to the ocean. It only got worse. It sounded like such a good idea to go in October to see the fall colors. We had packed up her tiny brown Toyota Celica and I got the impression she hadn't done a lot of camping. When I got hired at the Bothell Post Office she took to me like grease on a Ranch Drive-In cheeseburger. We became good enough friends to go camping together. Only snag was, that dirty dog, Tom Bell, sold her a cool tent and forgot to put the tent poles in the bag. We arrived at Lake Quilleuite campground around four in the afternoon and we started goofing off in the forest and hiking around the lake having a good old time. The sun went down around seven and we started to get cold. We built a small fire that didn't warm us up much so around nine we started putting up the tent and realized we had no tent poles. "No problem" I said, "We'll just use sticks. "By then it was pitch black out and we had forgotten flashlights. We were looking in the area we could see by the firelight. We found sticks all right. Bent, slimy old marshmallow sticks someone left behind. We slid the gooey sticks into her tent pole slots and got in our sleeping bags. It started raining. As the tent got heavier and heavier, the sticks kept bending closer and closer to our faces. When the tent was on our faces we gave up. We climbed into her tiny Toyota Celica, covered our wet selves with wet sleeping bags and tried to sleep. She was snoring in no time. But I'm afraid of the dark. AND we were the only ones in the campground.

Don't Pass That Smokey Brenda!

I could hear the siren. I just knew it. We were being pulled over in the middle of God Knows Where Texas. I had been busily studying my flashcards of airport codes as we crossed Texas on our way to Houston. I looked up and saw the state trooper car ahead and noticed Brenda was NOT slowing down. I yelled, "Don't pass that smokey Brenda!" I could predict exactly what she would say and I wasn't disappointed. "He's driving like an old grandma!" I mean, it was only eight hours ago that the truckers in Arizona had warned us to slow down in Texas or end up in jail. You'd think she was from Ballard the way she drives. So Brenda pulls over and the trooper is a lady. Next thing I know I'm peering out the back window of my hot red and black Rally Sport Camaro and Brenda is standing next to the trooper's car behind my car and I hear her say loudly, "Would you like a date?" She is holding out a sack of dates to the trooper and realizes that might sound funny to a woman. So she starts laughing really hard. Then she realizes we might end up in jail and starts sobbing hysterically. At that point I jumped out of the car and walked back to see if there was anything I could do, or in Brenda's case, undo. The trooper looks up at me and I see myself mirrored in her sunglasses. Brenda and I were wearing matching muu muus, baseball hats and alphabet shoes. I see her eyebrows raise a fraction of an inch. "Where are you girls from?" she asked me frowning. I told her we were from Seattle on our way to Houston so I could start flight attendant training the next day. At this point, I'm praying that we don't go to jail. I had only applied for five years and been rejected five dozen times before I got hired and I'm thinking, "This is not happening." "A $160.00 ticket later, we were on our way, and I was driving.

Old Ladies Catching Ducks

I looked out the window of my little trailer house and saw my friend Ruthie's small blue car. I dashed down my steps, and into my carport, and gathered up our gear: Life-jackets, paddles, duck bread, huge salmon net and a pillowcase to put the duck in. I greeted Ruthie and as we walked to the river I asked her if she had ever been canoeing before. "When I was a kid like you." she replied and I pondered if I was thirty she must be seventy. We got to the small marina and I loaded our gear into my canoe and I climbed in and held my end steady so she could get in. Apparently Ruthie had forgotten about getting into a canoe straight down while holding the dock. I looked at her with horror as her one leg went in the boat and the other stayed on the dock and the boat decided to go straight out in the water! Just as I thought her brown polyester slacks would split and she'd go in the drink, she managed to flip herself into the canoe. Whew. We paddled out into the Sammamish river and I asked, "What kind of duck do you want?" Ruthie looked at the dozens of ducks surrounding us as we tossed out the bread and said, "My female that died was brown and I'd like that one right there. My male duck is so heartbroken and he needs a new mate." I slowly lowered the huge salmon net into the water while

Ruthie tossed loads of bread over it. The pretty all-brown female was engrossed with the bread and I carefully positioned the net under her. BAM! I flipped the net and hauled her in and managed to transfer her to the pillow case without flipping us over. We paddled hard to the dock and I told Ruthie she needed to open her trunk right away and go home with that duck. Later that night the phone rang and it was Ruthie. I asked her how her duck was and she said, "Brownie is happy as a clam and my old male is even happier." Ducks in love…

Isn't That Called Breaking and Entering?

Thoughts of being in jail crossed my mind as I listened to Ruthie on the phone. I look awful in orange and had to interject, "Um, Ruthie, isn't that called Breaking and Entering?" To which she replied, "You just told me they are tearing down all those houses near you kid!" I'm not known for good judgment but at seventy-five I trusted her. At least she had lived a long time and that showed some smarts. Ruthie pulled up in front of my house in her gutless little pale blue Ford Tempo and got out wearing an outfit nearly identical to Emma Peel's in The Avengers. I went out in jeans and boots & an old flannel shirt and greeted her and nodded at the house next door. We looked all around and crept to the back door of the vacant house. I pulled out my masking tape and made a little square on the glass of the back door. Ruthie's eyes widened and she whispered loudly, "Whatrya doin there kid?" I tapped on the glass with a heavy pair of pliers and the square fell out. "I saw a burglar do this on Rockford Files one time." I reached in and unlocked the door and we crept into the musty vacant house. "Look at all this treasure kid!" Ruthie exclaimed as she saw intact light bulbs and light plates. We crept up the creaky old stairs and she filled up her pillowcase with moldy magazines as excited as a kid trick-or-treating. We heard a loud creak from downstairs and froze. We were frozen for ten minutes before we decided it must just be a rat roaming around. We crept down the squeaky stairs and non-chalantly walked back to my house and she placed the bag in the back seat of her car. She smiled at me and gripped my arm with her long, claw-like nails digging into me. Her eyes blazed with greed as she gave me a squeeze and said, "I'm ready for that old barn now." She took another pillowcase from her car and we walked casually along 175th towards the Kenmore club house. The four little empty ramblers looked dark and forlorn. We went down the long driveway to the huge white barn nestled down in the swamp and my skin started crawling. We slipped inside the open door and went about ten feet before I tripped on a piece of wood on the floor. A eerie scratching noise above us started and then rats began to fall from the old hayloft in clumps, raining down all around us. We both started shrieking and running and that ended Ruthie’s bad idea.

The Coincidental Sweater That Wasn't

Part of the job description for being my best friend, is helping me to shop. I hate shopping for clothes! To me, clothes are what you cover yourself with to avoid being arrested for indecent exposure. Luckily, my best friend Brenda is a clothes-horse. I'm always shocked when I look at her closet and she can't believe I only own two pairs of jeans. The summer of 2010 we had our 35th year Roosevelt high school reunion. I had bought a dress previously, but I needed cute shoes. Brenda was in town to visit her family so I asked her for help. I needed an expert. We got up to Bothell to The Alligator Purse and started browsing the racks. I was looking at sweaters and couldn't believe my eyes. I shouted to Brenda, who was a few racks away, "Look! They have a sweater EXACTLY like the one I donated to St. Vincent De Paul three years ago! What a coincidence!" Brenda walked over, stood close to me, and kicked me in the shins under the clothes rack. My eyes filled with tears of pain and shock. "Shhhhh!" She whispered. "I just put that there." It dawned on me that my best friend was up to no good. Again. I found some darling black leather high-heeled, backless shoes with black leather roses on top and was pretty excited. They even had fake leopard spot linings! When we got in my mini van and I asked Brenda what on earth she was doing with my gray Winnie the Pooh sweater. Turns out that after I put it on my front porch in my donation bag three years ago, she loved it so much that she snuck it out without telling me. She didn't want me to know that she had worn it three years. Then when she got tired of it, she had smuggled it into The Alligator Purse to get rid of it. My silly best friend.

Christmas at the Nudie Spa

Well this was a bit awkward. As I walked to my cubby in the main soaking room there were about five dozen women in ONLY their birthday suits. I hadn't seen that many naked women in one spot since my Eckstein junior high PE class in 1971. My fear of being the only old, well-rounded person at the day spa evaporated instantly as I saw I had the most common shape. We were a happy group of naked strangers ranging anyhere from one hundred twenty to four hundred pounds! My pal Mary was at her massage so I climbed in the hottest Jacuzzi pool and whispered "Hello" to my naked bench neighbor. Amber proceeded to tell me her life story, in its entirety, in ten minutes. I smiled and nodded and was happy my husband had trained me to listen without EVER having the expectation of getting a word in edgewise. She was delightful. I saw it was time for my massage and dried off and found the lounge area. It was filled with a huge semi-circular couch of robed, shower-capped women, reminding me of sea lions draped on the docks at Edmonds ferry dock. I requested a neck/shoulder/scalp massage and was happily surprised that someone invented a scalp massage. The rule of whispering was fairly well respected so when my half hour was up I exited to the lounge area and smiled and waved in giant motions with both hands to Mary, who was sitting next to the Christmas tree. Only it wasn't Mary and I did not have my glasses. Everyone looked alike in their spa robes and shower caps! Mary came from another room and found me and we tried the salt room. The huge floor was salt covered with a giant cloth with salt-filled pillows. The walls were bricks of Himalayan salt bricks of golden colors with lights shining gently through them from the back. (So the sign said, but I swear I saw them on Home Depot.com) It was lovely to lay down but embarrassing to have to flip ourselves over to all fours to get back up again. We were both hungry and had a delightful lunch at the spa cafe wearing our robes and shower caps with the rest of our nudie gang. As we went back to the hot tub room, Mary whispered to me, "Have you tried the mugworts splash?" It sound like something from Harry Potter so I followed her to a trough filled with what looked like hot swamp water. We poured it from big wooden bowls over ourselves, then over each others backs and then went to soak again. Totally happy and completely gumbified, we went home.

CBS or Cold Butt Syndrome

So last week I called Brenny and told her I had CBS. She said, "Oh, I love The Big Bang Theory!" I didn't know what that was but I said, "No, no, no. I have Cold Butt Syndrome. "She said, "Me too and I have CFS also." "You got a job at Central Forwarding System?! I worked there in '77!" "No, no, no." She said. "I have Cold Feet Syndrome." I told her a girl from high school said she had CNS. "Do you think she has Cold Nose Syndrome?" I asked. "Maybe she meant Cold knees Syndrome and can't spell." I guess we'll never know.

Chapter Eleven

Relatives

The Cat Who Was Scared Shitless

The sun was shining as we sat on the raised edge of the boardwalk trail. My sister Pam and I were cooking cornmeal mush for lunch & enjoying the little meadow surrounded by trees before the last ridge and descent to Cape Alava. It had been fun to hitch-hike to Shi Shi beach and at fifteen and seventeen we were six feet tall and bulllet-proof. The only minor setback was the Hoh River had been too high to forge & the tide had come in and trapped us on a dirt ledge for six hours. We were back in the saddle of our summer adventure as we waited for lunch. A cheerful looking young hippie couple emerged from the forest we had just left and asked to sit with us while they had lunch. The man said, "Whew, that was a close one man. We saw the ranger and thought we'd get busted for bringing our pet into the park." Pam and I looked all around for a dog but didn't see one. Then we noticed the side of one of the backpacks was moving around and we heard a muffled howling noise. The young lady squatted down and opened the pack and a cat came flying out along with the most hideous odor EVER. Pam looked over at me and said, "That cat was scared shitless!"

The Christmas Tree Which Fell From the Sky

In 1998, after Teddy was born, money became a little bit tight. To invest in frugality, my sister Pam and I hatched a plan to pick up artificial Christmas trees. It was a cold sunny day and we were cruising out 522 towards the Woodinville Ernst store, which was having a big sale on fake trees. I was driving my little navy blue Ford tempo when Pam shouted, "Gretch! A tree!" I saw it and pulled over next to the highway and couldn't believe my eyes. A seven foot tall gorgeous noble fir that would have been fifty bucks at Yakima Fruit stand, was lying at the side of the highway. I raised my arms high to the sky and shouted, "THANK YOU JESUS!" Then sissy and I spent ten minutes wrestling the tree into the tiny trunk of my car and tying it down. Just as we had climbed in the car, a small tan pick-up truck came roaring up the highway behind us and a middle-aged woman with wild long blond hair jumped out and started shouting. "My tree! My tree!" We got out and apologized and untied the tree and helped her load it into the back of her little truck. She was so happy. Pam and I bought our artificial trees and when Terry got home from work he said, "Take it back! I hate fake trees!" So I took it back with much chagrin that he didn't appreciate my rare attempt at serious long-term frugality. Five years later on

December 15th, Terry turned to me and said, "Where did you put that fake tree?" I stared at him with open-mouth disbelief. "We could save a lot of money if we used that." He said.

When Willard Lived in Kenmore

Pam and I were picking fat juicy blackberries on a hot sunny day in September down in the swamp. She said, "Hey, look Gretch, there's Betty's old shed. I walked over to where she was and could just barely make out the outline of the shape of the shed through the brambles. I said, "I thought the county tore that down when they bought this property for the park." I edged in closer and could see the door and said, "Come on sis, maybe there is some cool farm stuff inside." We slowly pushed the old door open and she followed me in. It was pitch black and we had come inside from the bright sun and we temporarily blinded. We could hear them before we could see them. The ceiling and walls started moving as hundreds of tiny scratching feet took off running in all directions and falling off the ceiling. "RATS!" I screamed. I nearly knocked sissy down trying to get out of that shed.

Chapter Twelve

Odds and Ends

I Was the Table Leaf Holder

"Are you okay Gretch?!" My sister Pam yelled from somewhere above as she and my brother-in-law Al held the sides of the antique table with the hopes that I would not be crushed from the weight. I was laying on the dining room floor, on my back, trying to keep the two sides of the heavy table from falling as Pam and Al secured the leaf in place. I had one foot on each of the sides and finally felt the weight ease up as the metal rungs were slid into place. "I'm fine!" I shouted up through the thick wood. Antiques. I only like them in museums or the homes of other people. This old table weighed more than my first car and it was a 1968 solid steel Volvo sedan from Ravenna Motors. While I was grateful to have a dining room table for our first Christmas in our new house in 1992, it was fairly terrifying for the five years I had to put the in the leaf.

You're NOT My Grandma!

The little baby sat happily on her beach blanket playing with her toys. Her limp beach ball was her run-a-way favorite and I swear it looked like she kept trying to blow it up. Heloise was only six months old, with dark blue eyes and light brown wispy hair. She had on a blue checked sundress with matching bucket hat that covered her little head to her chin. There is a gap when your children are grown, before you get grandchildren that can make you crazy. All of a sudden that old biological clock starts ringing and you crave babies. Smart design we have, reinforced by mirrors showing every wrinkle, that create a desire for immortality, through grandchildren. Terry started it by mentioning that the people in the cabin next to us had a really cute baby. The day before I had seen three baby raccoons, three baby sea otters and one spotted baby deer. I was in a baby frenzy after that. I saw the young couple walking to the resort whale-viewing bench and grabbed a cup of coffee and non-chalantly followed them down there. I admired their baby, and casually mentioned had two children, was a school teacher, had been a scout leader for ten years...Anything to sell my trustworthiness… because I wanted to babysit! The next day as we left for a bike ride I stopped at their cabin to see if they might like to take our canoe for a spin to see the seals and their pups in the bay up close and of course I could watch the baby right there on the beach where they could see her at all times. So back to the beach. Heloise played with her beach ball, then four different rattles and we were having a wonderful time. She could even say, "Goo!" After a half hour I leaned over to pass her the pacifier. Quick as a lightning she snatched my sunglasses off my face and stared into my eyes. Her deafening howl said "You're NOT my grandmother!" Busted. Luckily, her mom and dad were on their way into the beach and I only had to have my ears pierced for five minutes. That Eloise! She is one smart baby.

The Summer of Seventeen Snakes

I am not a big fan of snakes. Now that I'm older, they startle me. After working on the pristine cruise ship, I decided to beautify my yard. The only snag was, I hadn't done any yard work in the front yard for twenty years and it looked like hell. One sunny afternoon the first week of August, I came down my mom's wheelchair ramp and hung over the railing to get an idea of where to start working the next day. The ground was moving. Why was the ground moving? I stared at the unruly weeds and saw a snake. Well, that was okay. One snake. Then I looked more closely and saw two. Finally, I counted ten! No big deal I thought, I'm brave, and I can deal with it. The next morning I forgot all about them and came sauntering down the ramp to my mini van and nearly stepped on one! Sassy little snake with attitude. It gave me the look I give my kids when I'm sunbathing in my lawn chair with a Jackie Collins novel and they try to disturb me. It didn't even hurry off. I had to stomp at it before it would it slither down between the wooden slats of the ramp. That's when I noticed the hole. Turns out that left undisturbed, the snakes had made a nest under the wheelchair ramp. So now that I had inadvertently created a snake condo, how on earth was I going to get rid of them? Kids! Best form of cheap labor ever created. Luckily, Troy hadn't found a summer job and needed a way to fund his Arizona Ice Tea addiction. I hired him to catch and relocate the snakes up to Wallace Creek Swamp Park. He was good at it too! Every afternoon when I'd be working in the yard, when he'd hear me screaming, he'd dash out and fill up his pillowcase with the slimy little friends and drive them off to the park for a mere two bucks a snake. Best investment in my mental health I ever made! Now I had only counted ten snakes that first day and two weeks later, Troy had caught thirteen, so I was feeling pretty cocky about working in my ugly little yard. Then a teenage snake showed up and I yelled for Troy and he made short work of catching it and taking off with it for the park. Then I saw her. The BIG MOMMY snake. Three feet long and wide around as a roll of quarters. She was heading for the hole under the ramp. I fought my fright and grabbed my rake, ran up the ramp and leaned over the railing to block her path. Where was Troy?! He'd been gone twenty minutes! We were at a stand off. Four times she approached the ramp as the sun was lowering. She wanted to go to bed. I carefully fended off her attempts by leaning over and moving the rake. She was getting crafty and starting to approach from the sides. After a half hour she backed up and coiled up. I was ready, gripping the rake with two hands leaning over the railing staring her down. She sprang at the rake and attacked it! It all happened so fast! When she hit the hard green plastic rake at full force, it was at a slight angle, and she shot right up the rake handle at my face! I screamed and threw the rake and it landed with mommy snake under the pine tree in the weeds. My adrenaline was making me shake all over. The van! Troy was back! He got out and I begged him to catch her and make one more trip to the park. He did. Teddy and Carlos were with him in the van and as he pulled out of the driveway I could see him passing the snake bag to the back seat for Teddy to hold. As the bag brushed Carlos's shoulder in the front seat, I could hear screaming from the van as it went down the road. I'm not the only one afraid of snakes.

You Know You Are a Really Bad Housekeeper When...

1 You take your long-handled duster to one corner of the ceiling and your youngest child shouts, "Mom! What are you doing?!" "If you take down those black cobwebs our house won't look like Halloween year round!"

2 You train your oldest son to clean his bathroom when he is eight years old and feel proud of him. You open the shower curtain to check how the tub looks for his eighteenth birthday and realize you forgot to tell him the cleaning the bathtub was part of the job.

3 You clean your pantry and find thirty-two tiny bags of coffee from coffee makers from hotels going back to 1987.

4 You spend two hours cutting open the tiny coffee bags and putting them in your canister.

5 You realize you will never get those two hours back.

6 You clean your closet and find your missing address book and decide to write your best friend a letter.

7 You find $20.00 that you hid for emergencies behind the stamps in the address book and decide:

Being a bad housekeeper isn't all bad.

The Pee Tree

Patty smiled as she looked at my lattice and my small Nelly Moser clematis climbing it. "You and Brenda did a good job on the lattice but you really need to give these little hedge trees some Miracle Gro Gretchen. Look, this whole side is dying and it looks awful." I looked at the little cone-shaped tree with only one green branch on the bottom. The brown Charlie Brown tree is six feet high. I'm partial to dead branches so I had planted a few more white and pink Nelly's to climb it. I grimaced and said, "That's the Pee Tree." "When Owen and I went to plug up the Norwegian Tunnel Rat holes we smelled something. Turns out Terry had been peeing on my trees for five years. I pointed to a beauty bark lined hole and said, "See, look, I dug him a pee hole and he promised to use it so I think there is hope for the Pee Tree."

My Office Really Stinks

I clicked the Play Video icon on my friend's Facebook page and stared at the beautiful pheasant walking in his back yard. When we moved to Kenmore in 1990, I'd see pheasants in the meadows along the river. That was before my sister's dog ran loose and chased them away. I found pheasant chicks on Craigslist and built a small pen of cardboard with a tarp bottom and chicken wire top. I called Brenny to see if she'd go to the feed store with me. We picked up all the gear they told us we needed and on May 16th 2012 we picked up my eleven ten day old chicks. They were tiny and fuzzy and very cute. What I didn't know was that they would stink. Eye-burning stink. I didn't care though. Then they quadrupled in size in a week and lost their downy coats. I left the chicken-wire top off their pen when I dashed for water and five had flown the coop. They were on the windowsill pecking at the glass trying to get out. I got them back in the pen and gave them corn on the cob and juicy watermelon. When they got a treat they liked to trill. Just like the Tribbles on Star Trek. The rest of the time they went peep, peep, peep. After six weeks the air in my office was so rancid your eyes would burn walking in. When I tried to change the newspaper in the bottom of the pen they kept flying out. Finally it was time for them to live in my yard. As Bren and I tipped the carrier to the pen, the pheasants shot straight up into the air never to be seen again. The odor never left the little office in our house. We finally had to paint over the smell.

Are You Really Hitchhiking?

The SUV slowed down as it crossed the dusty parking lot and the window came down. I tried so hard to pin on a winning smile. "Are you really hitchhiking?" Asked the cute young brunette, who might not be used to seeing sixty-year old ladies thumbing it. "I sure am." I said. "My feet won't go one more foot since we hiked the whole Perimeter Trail." I heard the two young gals and older lady in the back exclaim to each other. "If ya'll don't mind a cuddle, climb in back with the baby." I climbed in with baby Carter and told them how we missed a turn on the "easy" trail and ended up following a goat trail a thousand feet straight up a cliff and the extra six vertical miles of terror ruined me. They were sympathetic to my plight and took me to Main Street. I pointed at the three block hill to Brenny's and thanked them for the ride. Well, those ladies from Mustang Island Texas would have none of that and dropped me off right at Brenda's door. They said the town near them was called, "Hitch-Up" because so few people had cars to start with. I went to watch the convention with Tom and Brenda. Terry showed up a few minutes later. He got lost on another trail after I bailed out on him. He joined us in the TV room and Bren and I couldn't believe it. Hillary Clinton had won the candidacy so we snuck out to the front porch and started banging pots and pans as hard as we could. They live on a hill so we were certain the entire town of Ouray heard us. They weren't the only ones. Tom and Terry ran out to find out what was happening and couldn't believe would cause such a ruckus. Well, duh... The next day Tom fired up the tiny Toyota 4X4 and Bren and I poured our considerable selves into the miniscule jump seats behind them and off we went. The only thing scarier than hiking vertically is driving vertically. I thought I might throw up down the back of Terry's shirt and ended up holding hands with Bren most of the way since it seemed clear to me that it would be my last chance. Bullion King Lake is at 12,000 feet elevation and the parking lot was at 9,000. We stilled needed to hike that last thin-air mile but I was fairly inspired by being able to throw snow balls at Terry. Tom caught all the fish caught and I felt bad for Terry but he wasn't riding the jump seat like a pretzel, so not too bad. Terry and I went over to Silverton the next day with the thought of taking the steam train down to Durango, but we got sidetracked driving up Mineral Creek Valley and staring at campgrounds. It was so pretty, we stopped to take a picture, which was huge mistake. The minute we opened the doors, we were swarmed by horseflies, mosquitoes and No-see-ums. Many bites later, we arrived in Silverton only to see the train on its way to Durango. We decided to tour the world's biggest mining museum cut our losses. The equipment for drilling holes to insert the dynamite was impressive and I said to Terry, "Hold that thing between your legs like you know what to do with it." I snapped a cute picture of Terry pretending to operate the drill. After three days at Tom and Brenda's we moved over to the Wiesbaden resort in downtown so we wouldn't wear out our welcome. We decided to pick up some food for Tom and Brenda to replenish what we had blasted through while staying with them. The town of Ridgeway, which has the only store near Telluride, reflected that Ralph Lauren shopped there. Terry's face turned so pale and I thought he was having a heart attack, but it was only Price Shock. He held up a can of coffee, which was $18.00,!(We buy the same thing at Kenmore Grocery Outlet for six dollars) The Wiesbaden was idyllic except instead of a wall clock we had a giant thermometer. We never knew what time it was, and we didn't care.

Face Broth

I snuggled down into my folded electric blanket and opened my latest historical romance novel by Lisa Kleypas. The heat from the blanket on "H" above and below me relaxed me instantly. I couldn't see the words. Was I going blind?! I removed my reading glasses and held them to the light and realized I had a thick oil slick going on. Oops. After five tries of making homemade, chemical free beauty cream I had finally gotten it right. Almost. (Never try to moisturize and read the same night) My sister is starting a lotion/potion business and had given me her recipe. Only snag was that I have never followed a recipe in my entire life. Just don't have the patience for details. I ordered the shea butter and coconut butter online then told Brenda what I was doing. She added many suggestions until I had added glycerin, rose hip seed oil, aloe vera, elastin and hyaluronic acid. My only addition was almond extract. (Maybe needed almond oil but bought what Kookmore Safeway had to offer.) On my first try I used my sister's recipe and watched the DIY (Do It Yourself) video on Youtube. Seemed easy enough and I was very excited in the morning to slather some on my face. I opened the jar and stuck my finger in and was confronted by a rock hard combination of ingredients that DID NOT stay whipped together. I poked harder and the top crust broke and my finger was covered in blue goo. I poured some of that in my hand and slopped it on my face and arms and legs thinking I'd probably look sixteen after it soaked in. Instead I felt sticky. The phone rang and I told Brenda I had accidentally made face broth and for some reason I was turning blue and was very sticky. She asked if I had read the labels knowing darn well I hadn't. I went upstairs and found some clean glasses and read, "Hyaluronic acid dietary supplement in pure blueberry juice."

What Vacuum Cleaner?

"What vacuum cleaner?" I said to my new handy-woman Pepper Fox. She gave me a blank look. "I got rid of it four years ago when I got a job. "Her eyebrows raised slightly and she said, "You don't own a vacuum cleaner?" I looked back at her and said, "When I got a job I got a cleaning lady and she vacuums." Pepper looked doubtfully at my carpet which had about three gallons of orange cat hair strewn everywhere.

"I can only afford her every other week." I said slightly guiltily. I went on to tell her what I had learned from Alexander-McCall Smith through his character, Isabel Dalhousie, in his book, "The Sunday Philosophers Club." Pepper stared at me with mild disbelief that I would alter my life from some fictional book I read so I explained myself. "According to Isabel Dalhousie, people with jobs are obligated to hire people with jobs that help them." I walked over to the tiny apron cupboard and pulled out the broom and handed it to her and said with a smile, "Here you go." She took the broom and said to me with a gleam in her eye, "I don't think this thing will hold both of us."

47916804R00100

Made in the USA
Columbia, SC
04 January 2019